Messages from the Masters

Messages
from the
Masters

Timeless Truths for Spiritual Seekers

Richard Andrew King

Library of Congress Cataloging-in-Publication Data

King, Richard Andrew
Messages From The Masters
ISBN: 978-0-931872-07-5
Date of Publication: 12 December 2011

DEDICATION

To my beloved Master,
Maharaj Charan Singh Ji,
and for his endless love,
protection, guidance and grace.

Acknowledgments

Many thanks to KC Thomas for his query
and support for this work.

Thanks also to Shannon Yarbrough,
author of Stealing Wishes,
for his cover design.

Many thanks, also, to graphic artist Liana Moisescu
in assisting with the hardcover.

Richard Andrew King
PO Box 3621
Laguna Hills, CA 92654-3621
www.RichardKing.net

Messages from the Masters
Timeless Truths for Spiritual Seekers

Table of Contents

Author's Introduction

In many ways this is a dangerous book to read. There are two paths we can take in life: the worldly path and the spiritual path. The former is a known commodity. It is familiar; comfortable. The latter, although universal and timeless, is not generally a known commodity. It is unfamiliar and may be uncomfortable to comprehend in the beginning. Yet, it holds the greatest of truths for those hungry souls seeking spiritual solace and nectar.

These paths of the world and the spirit are diametrically opposed; their goals irreconcilable. The spiritual path runs counter to the entire gamut of attitudes, philosophies and ideals of the modern world. Thus, the concepts presented here may be totally foreign, even antagonistic, to thoughts of earthly life held dear. Yet, the messages shared here have nothing to do with earthly life. They have everything to do with spiritual life, spiritual pursuits, spiritual goals. And that's the point. Such contrasting philosophies can create turmoil to a mind entrenched in worldly ways and means, shake it up and cause it to question as it never has before. Such a process is by its very nature uncomfortable. But that is the precise purpose of the Masters' messages and teachings - to awaken the sleeping soul from its eons-old slumber and liberate it from the dense darkness of matter and materialism and ultimately take it Home.

Contrarily, the messages herein may be extremely comfortable, reassuring and inspirational, resonating within the deepest depths of the soul and its longing for a greater truth than the world can possibly know, let alone offer, a truth of spiritual liberation and soul salvation, a truth that ultimately brings eternal peace and everlasting bliss.

As these messages are read, even hopefully studied, grasped and lived, it will be helpful to realize that even though many are quite direct and may seem harsh on the surface, they are meant for the individual's highest and best spiritual good, not his worldly good but the good that cuts the cords and severs the chains of attachment to a dense material world that is deeply dark, foreboding, and incarcerating, enslaving the soul in an insufferable and seemingly eternal dungeon of blindness, pain, suffering, sorrow and unspeakable limitation. Masters do not come to make our worldly life comfortable, joyful or successful. Just the opposite. Their job is to make us uncomfortable so we turn our heads and redirect our consciousness inward and upward to where we will one day not only be free but be everlastingly grateful for the timeless messages the Masters bring.

In Love, Life and Light,

Richard Andrew King

Messages from the Masters

Chapter One

IN SEARCH OF TRUTH

Looking for answers in your search for spiritual Truth? Tired of hitting dead ends? Exhausted in following this road and that road only to be disappointed at what you found or didn't find? Are you worn out from seeking philosophies, religions or courses of study that don't measure up to spiritual, ethical or moral ideals, that violate spiritual laws, that leave you with more questions than answers, more distrust than trust? Are you feeling that there's more to life than what you currently know but you don't know where to look or with whom to talk to find the answers you seek? Are you tired of the nonsense going on in the world? Perhaps even fed up with it? Are you disillusioned with life in general, feeling an emptiness and longing for something you know exists but which you can't put your finger on? Are you tired of transient relationships that leave you spent, betrayed, angry, lost, confused? Are you lonely for spiritual nectar? Are you just plain lonely? Need peace, happiness and tranquility in your life? Have you heard about vegetarianism, karma, reincarnation, meditation and want to know more about these concepts and why they are such an intricate and critical aspect of the spiritual path and lifestyle? Or do you simply feel a pull, a tugging at your soul, a restless, pressing, impatient urging to seek God?

These are some of the reasons leading people to the Spiritual Path. Something is definitely missing in their lives, and though they may not know what it is, they search, sometimes for years, sometimes for decades, sometimes even for an entire lifetime. Then, through some quirk of fate, they bump into a person who says something or does something that strikes a chord in them, a chord of truth, a chord which excites them, a chord whose mellifluous melodies they want to hear again, a chord which resonates deeply in the very center of their soul, a chord which, like a powerful magnate, draws them helplessly closer to the source, a chord which makes them want to know more, a chord that tells them instinctively they've found what they've been looking and longing for, an irresistible chord so powerfully real they begin to tear up with joy for this is the chord of the Lord. He has come for them to take them Home, and deep in their psyches they know it. If any of this rings true with you, read on. If not, you probably won't be reading this sentence anyway.

Messages from the Masters

Truth

There is truth and then there is Truth. There are teachers and then there are Teachers. There are masters and then there are Masters. This book is about spiritual Masters and the messages they share with humanity; the Truth they bring to the world and to those who have ears to *hear*, eyes to *see* and hearts filled with genuine longing for what is real and eternal.

Masters are the Sons of God. Obviously this is hard to believe, and I'm not asking you to believe it. In fact, you shouldn't. Take nothing for granted just because it's written in a book. Put it to the test. Prove it for yourself. However, if your search has been fair, true and unbiased; if your search has led you to conclusions based, not on someone else's opinions, philosophies and experiences but your own; if you have devoted enough time, effort, energy, thought and concentration upon this matter and given one-hundred percent to actually following the teachings of Masters and living the lifestyle they suggest, then you will, indeed, come to the same conclusion. It would be impossible not to. Masters are the Sons of God incarnate.

Spiritual Truth endures. It doesn't change. It carries the same message from millennia to millennia, civilization to civilization, culture to culture, nation to nation. Truth has no alliance with fads or faces, kings or queens, presidents or paupers, nations or nabobs, celebrities or cosmopolites, or special interest groups with self-serving, worldly agendas. Truth is the same today as it was yesterday and will be tomorrow. From time immemorial, truth is truth and does not change.

Because of their divine status and nexus, it is Masters who bring spiritual Truth to the world. Regardless of their nationality, their worldly occupation or their language, the Truth they espouse is always the same: God is real. He exists. Man, who is the highest form of creation, can know Him, realize Him, be one with Him _if_ he makes himself worthy of Him, and he can do all of this while he is alive. In fact, the only time man can know God, be one with Him and thereby gain his Salvation, is when he occupies the human form, the penultimate gift of God. The ultimate gift is Initiation by a Perfect Master into the mysteries of life.

The Truths Masters bring are profound. In fact, some of these truths may shock the individual, giving him great pause to ponder. These Truths will often revolutionize a person's life, sometimes shaking it to the core in order to make the person wake up so that his illusions of the world are shattered and he can be freed from this negative dark dimension of duality, destruction, decay and death where souls circle and cycle in endless turmoil and tears for endless years and lives.

Masters, also called Saints and/or Perfect Saints, pull no punches. They tell it like it is, often shooting straight from the hip and taking no prisoners because, in fact, their job is to free prisoners from _this_ world,

Messages from the Masters

liberate them from ignorance, illusion, delusion and humiliating captivity, thus reinstating them on the altar of their divine heritage. The only way to do this is to teach and tell the Truth of life from their exalted palace of absolute spirituality.

Perfect Masters simply elucidate the Truth - dispassionately, calmly, lovingly. Even though they often pull no punches, they do not coerce or force. They simply share. Their job is to save souls from the clutches of this world, sever them from their attachments so they can be finally free from eons of bondage in this dark and nether dungeon we call the earth. Their compassion knows no bounds and their power knows no equal. They are the apotheosis of living perfection and embodiment of God.

Masters are not politicians. Nor do they concern themselves with that which is politically correct or passingly popular. Nor do they involve themselves with worldly affairs. Their only business is the spiritual business of soul salvation. They are universal by nature. They love all, favor none, play no games, seek no empires, cherish no celebrity, claim no status, never blow their own horn and walk upon the earth as if they were the greatest of sinners, all the time saving sinners from the nefarious clutches of this nether world.

Masters are the true givers of the universe, never holding their palms up or begging from others. They dedicate their lives to humanity. They do their own work, never take charity and demand their disciples do the same.

These Perfect Masters do not care about making the world a paradise or bringing peace to the world. The world is not supposed to be a paradise, will never be a paradise, nor will it ever have peace. Such is not the Creator's plan for this world. As Christ said in St. Matthew (10:34) - *Think not that I am come to bring peace on earth; I came not to send peace but a sword.* This is the same spiritual truth echoed by all perfect mystics. Their job, their assignment from God, is to sever the cords of attachment which bind souls to this world. Saints' swords sever cords saving souls from slavery.

Because Masters care about saving souls, they bring the sword of knowledge with them and sever the roots of those whose time it is to return Home. Ignorance, it has been said, is the root cause of the downfall of the soul. Unless that ignorance is destroyed, unless the soul is severed from its ignorance, it will continue to be enslaved for eons of time in a prison of profound suffering and sorrow. Man doesn't know this. Saints do, and that's why they exist on the earth. It's all about Salvation.

A Time for Saints

If ever there were a time for Saints to be in the world (and there is always, fortunately, at least one Saint present on the earth at all times), it is now. The world is degenerating and degrading at a rapid pace. The signs of this degeneration are universally extant and multiplying at ferocious speed. All it takes is a little spiritual sentience, a little awareness and a casual look 'round at the earth, its collective consciousness, its activities, its consumptions, its ideals, and its gross lack of spirituality to see that the world is, indeed, in great decay.

For example, take the number of laws on the books today. Can they all be counted? There are so many laws one wonders how our culture is not drowned under the sheer weight of their collective mass. What do these laws say about our civilization? They say it is not very civil at all. The number of laws on our books today is not a reflection of how civilized we are but how *uncivilized* we are.

Spiritually, there is only one law and that is the law of love. This is the operative law in God's upper kingdoms. It is the only law needed for a truly civilized society. When the law of love is embedded in the minds and hearts of all souls, there is no need for any other law whatsoever. Love only loves. Love only does good. When love is the only law on the books, no one would ever think, dream or take any action to hurt, harm, maim, injure, deceive or destroy another living soul in the most minute of ways. Therefore, dishonesty, anger, hatred, selfishness, theft, adultery, betrayal, greed, usury, duplicity, deceit, prevarication, vilification, denigration, misrepresentation, manipulation, and a million and one other forms of evil would not, could not, exist. Period. Hence, the number of laws in a society is directly proportional to the lack of spirituality in that society. The more laws, the less love, and the less a society is civilized. The number of laws on our cultural books today is a clear indication of how <u>un</u>civilized we are, not how civilized.

Another clear indication of the rapid degradation of the world is the amount of violence, especially killings, and more especially the killing of kids by kids! How unbelievably insane and inane is it for young children to walk into a school toting firearms of all makes and sizes and begin opening fire on other children and taking, nay, destroying, lives upon lives? What kind of maniacal madness is this? How embarrassingly ludicrous is this also for any civilization, any culture, any country, any establishment, any body to allow this type of vicious and murderous predation to not only occur but continue? Is this the school's problem? No. It's society's problem. These children have been fed, by 'adults,' enormous masses of rich and varied violence throughout their lives in the forms of movies, television shows, video games, magazines, books, and a whole host of people who believe it's acceptable to promote this banal and baneful barbarism. It's no wonder these kids, *kids*, are coming unglued at the seams and going absolutely ballistic. They're doing so because society is coming unglued at its seams and is literally going ballistic itself. The behavior of these children is nothing but a mirror of adult mores and values. Unspeakable.

The incredulously sad part of this violence is the lack of accountability and responsibility on the part of the 'adults' creating, marketing, promoting and selling such horrific ideas, products and services as if indulgence in such things were fun and pleasurable! Kids copy adults. If adults think and conduct themselves in such a way as to not only accept violence but promote and glorify it, the kids will follow suit. This is not rocket science. This is life science, and it's pretty simple. Good begets good. Evil begets evil. Kindness begets kindness. Peace begets peace. Love begets love. Hate begets hate, and violence surely and most painfully and sorrowfully, begets violence and all of the tragedy, turmoil, tribulation, tears, suffering, sorrow and agonizing pain associated with it. Yet, 'adults' continue to promote this barbaric insanity in the form of entertainment, arguing that it serves as a release from the craziness of the world. If this kind of pernicious activity were not promoted in the first place, there would be no craziness in the world. Whatever happened to good wholesome fun?

The prolific and unrestrained usage and indulgence of recreational drugs and alcohol in our world is yet another indication of the world's degeneracy. Life is hard enough without complicating it with a plethora of provocative poisons and destructive delights. Yet, that's what's happening. Again, one of the empty and indefensible arguments for the ingestion of such devious and demonic substances is the escape from reality they presumably offer. Such malevolent machinations. These poisons obliterate reality, imbed and inculcate illusion and simply ruin lives, often destroying them in the process. How can these diabolical contaminants bring pleasure when the end result of their use is addiction, pain, sorrow, suffering, turmoil, tragedy, tears, decay, disease, destruction and death? People say they want peace and happiness in their lives and yet they freely ingest themselves with the pestilential poisons insuring and guaranteeing their sorrow, suffering, misery and madness. Where is the common sense in this behavior?

Deceit is a main contributor to our society's decay. Who can be trusted anymore? Who doesn't have some hidden agenda to promote and fulfill? Who is not so saturated with money, lust, power, fame, name and celebrity that they'll doing anything to get it, even sacrifice their ethics or other people's reputations or lives in the process? In fact, do people have a code of ethics to live by anymore? Codes of ethics, it seems, have found their way into museums, taking their place along side the latest dinosaur exhibit. And what contract is so clear and simple that one doesn't need a lawyer to interpret it? How small does small print have to be? And how hidden? And what about that huge bag of potato chips on the counter? It looks great, right? Until you open it. Then you can almost count the number of chips in the bag on one hand while having to have a hand full of money in the other hand to pay for it.

Thankfully, Masters do not deceive. They're straight shooters. Deceit is foreign to who they are. One may take issue with what they say (an unfortunate mishap) and not like what they say but one can never question the ethics of Saints, of Perfect Masters. They're impeccable - both the Saint and his ethics. You can take that to the bank, hopefully the bank of your soul.

Another redline indicator of our degenerating earth is the rampant and rabid explosion of sexual indulgence, indulgence which has lost all sight and understanding of spiritual law, violating it without a breath of conscience or a concern for its consequences. One of the Saints quoted in this work is Kabir, a Perfect Master of the 15th and 16th Centuries. He said,

Sex indulgence is the lowest of human activities. That men should be at all proud of it surpasses understanding. Do not all the animals indulge in it? Sex indulgence saps our physical vitality, weakens our mental power, and above all, it seriously hampers our spiritual progress. For spiritual progress one has to travel upwards. Sex indulgence does the opposite. It uses the power of the Word (God's Energy) *in the lowest of human activities.*

Yet, our culture not only regards sexuality as a thing of which to be proud, but it also rewards, promotes and glorifies it as though to be a sex symbol were the apotheosis of achievement in this world. The promotion and glorification of sex is everywhere you look: movies, magazines, television, books, billboards, advertisements, award shows, social celebrations and on and on and on. It is a truth that in our society sex sells. What does that say about us? It is also no less a truth that in our society sex destroys, but seldom is this aspect of sexuality ever mentioned. If it were, it wouldn't sell. How many individual's lives, well-beings, families, children, careers and reputations have been diseased, destroyed, ruined, shamed, dismantled, lost and besieged with turmoil and despair because of sex being out of control - physically, emotionally, psychologically, financially, socially? This is not to say sex is bad. Saints acknowledge it is a natural aspect of this creation. But its immense over-indulgence, glorification, consumption and inappropriate use is bad, at least for the soul as it strives to make headway on the spiritual path.

It is no mistake that halos have always been pictured throughout history around the heads of mystics, not their genitalia. Halos represent the purity of one's energy and connection with the God force which is manifested in man at the head level. As long as the soul is chained to the lower sexual outlets of his being, man's consciousness will never be able to rise to that level which is both hallowed and haloed. And since, as Saint Ravidas declares, *True happiness lies in realizing true holiness*, man will never find true happiness because he chooses not to lead a holy (pure) life but rather indulge in an unholy and impure one.

Another reason why the Messages from the Masters are so very needed today is the general gloom of the mass consciousness. Ever take a good hard look at the faces of models on magazine covers for instance? They're not happy faces, that's for sure. They're stern, dark, gloomy, lost, foreboding, almost lifeless. There is no vibrancy in them. No joy. No happiness. It's sad.

Yet, isn't that where the general mindset of our culture is these days? Lost? Confused? Bewildered? Distraught? Agonized? Disturbed? Angry? Unhappy? There are, of course, exceptions, but on the whole it would be a hard sell to make a case for our society being a happy, content and spiritual lot. Fortunately, Mystics bring messages of happiness and show people how to find that happiness. They realize more than anyone the absolute negativity of this dimension and the sad plight of the souls in it. That's why they come to save souls. It is solely out of their undying compassion for the suffering of humanity. If one follows their teachings and lives the life they recommend, any soul will not only gain happiness but also liberation from its enslavement in this dark and foreboding world. In Chapter Two we'll take a closer look at these Masters and the messages they bring to all of us who have ears to *hear*.

A Thousand Mile Journey

© Richard Andrew King

A thousand mile journey
begins with step the first,
but victory in the journey
is reflected in our thirst
to keep on taking steps,
even crawling in the dirt
when the sorrow of the journey
engulfs our heart with hurt.

One thousand miles of little steps
is a sojourn of travail.
Thunderstorms and hurricanes
as well as maelstroms prevail.
If this thousand mile journey
were easy, light and fun,
there would be more travelers
in this thousand mile run.

But few there are to dare the race.
Myopic comfort kills the dream.
Too long, too hard, too full of plight,
too many fears extreme
kill the hoping heart
and the will with little grit;
so this thousand mile journey
is challenged only by the fit.

So should it be, and rightly so--
for those who win the Prize
should be the ones undaunted
and full of triumph in their eyes.
Laurels only should be showered
on those within the field
with courage strong and vision long,
and spirits which never yield!

Chapter Two

MASTERS

I and my Father are one.
[*Holy Bible*: St. John 10:30]

And the Word was made flesh and dwelt among us.
[St. John 1:14]

The Master is the manifest form of the Lord.[1] Nothing else really need be said. Christ recognized this truth when he said: *I and my Father are one.* Emphasis here is given on the word, *one*. In *one* there are not two. In *one*, two does not exist; cannot exist. Hence, there is no division, duality, plurality, separation; nothing beyond *One*, i.e., *Oneness*. *One* is *God, God is One* and all Masters--all Perfect Masters, are Sons of God--His Divine Manifestation-- and there is absolutely no difference between God and the Perfect Master. *All Saints are Sons of God.*[2] They are *One* with God, and all Saints have declared this fact to be true.

In this text the word *Master* stands for the highest manifestation of God. It is synonymous with *Perfect Master, Living Master, Saint, Perfect Saint, Guru, and Sat Guru.* These words, for the purposes of this text, are interchangeable. Other saints, masters and gurus [teachers] do exist and have existed but as all things have levels and degrees of perfection, so do masters. While all saints are not *Perfect Saints*, so also not all masters are *Perfect Masters*; not all gurus are *Sat Gurus* [supreme teachers]. Thus, wherever used, the word *Master*, with a capital 'M', will designate the *Absolute Son of God in manifest form.*

This work brings to light divine messages from these Sons of God, i.e., *Messages From The Masters.* The purpose of Masters for being in the world is to awaken souls to their spiritually Divine heritage, to assist them in fulfilling *the* great and *sole* purpose of human life: achieving God-realization while *living* in the human body and *not waiting* to achieve this goal until after this precious life has been spent, i.e. after death, which, in fact, is an impossibility. In brief, Saints only come into this world to take us out of it, to take us back to the Lord.[3]

Although some religious belief is founded on the fact that only one Master has walked on the face of the earth, such is not the case. As Maharaj Charan Singh Ji, a Perfect Saint of the Twentieth Century, has declared: *In every age there has always been a Master, and in every age there will be a Master. . . There always has been a Master in the world.*[4]

Guru Nanak, a famous Saint of India who lived during the 15th and 16th Centuries, has commented on this concept of there being only one Master in the history of the world. He says:

> *God, who is just and all merciful, would not dispense His mercy in so capricious a manner. He would not confine His saints to a brief period and debar those born earlier or later from attaining salvation and union with Him. . . The Lord, in fact, has been all-merciful in His grace. He has so ordained that the world will never be without saints. This is a divine law which, unlike social or political laws, cannot be changed. Those who seek union with Him will always have a master to help and guide them.*[5]

And, of course, this makes perfectly logical sense. When we think of the gargantuan expanse of our universe with its untold number of galaxies, solar systems, suns, planets and other living beings, why would God, the infinite Creator of All, limit spiritual salvation to only those souls who lived on one insignificant little planet during a micro-flash of its life span and, thereby, summarily exclude every other living soul He created for all time--billions, even trillions, of years? No. It is not possible for an infinite God to be finite. In fact, it is really an insult to the power of God to presume He would manifest his love in such a random and limited manner. This is why He declares through all His Sons that the earth has never had just one Master. *In every age there has always been a Master, and in every age there will be a Master.*

It must be pointed out that *no Saint comes into the world to create any religion or to divide us or bind us to any organization or any particular religion. Saints come only to teach us spirituality.*[6] Saints also *do not come to raise our standard of living in this world. They come to set us free from this world and take us back to the Lord.*[7]

Additionally, all Saints are the *Word made flesh.* As St. John said of Christ Jesus: *And the Word was made flesh and dwelt among us* [St. John 1:14]. According to *Kabir*, another of India's most famous Perfect Saints and a contemporary of Guru Nanak, the *Word*, referenced by St. John, is not a lettered word but actually *God in dynamic action.*[8]

The *Word*, of course, has also been called many names by various Saints of different races, places and tongues throughout the ages. Its essence is universal, encompassing the teaching of all Perfect Masters who have recognized it as the *Voice of God.* Among the appellations for the *Word* are the following: *Audible Life Stream, Shabd, Nam, Nad, Kalma, Dhun, the Sound Current, Audible Life Stream, Celestial Music, and the Unstruck Melody* [see Chapter Nine: *Soul Food*].

Messages from the Masters

Maharaj Sawan Singh Ji, a Perfect Master of the early 1900s states: *The Word is the foundation on which the whole visible and invisible structure of the Universe is resting. Everything has sprung from this Word. The Master is the embodiment of this Word and is one with it.*[9] Being *one* with it, therefore, the *Master* and the *Word* are identical. They are God.

As we remember further from St. John: *In the beginning was the Word, and the Word was with God and the Word was God* [St. John 1:1]. As God is *the Father* and the *Word* is God, then the *Father* is the *Word*. Christ said: *I and my Father are one.* In other words, *I and the Word are one.* This is exactly what Perfect Master Maharaj Sawan Singh is saying--the *Master* is the *Word of God*; the *Master is God*.

This is further corroborated by Maharaj Charan Singh who says: *Our real Master is the Word, Logos, Shabd, Nam, the Audible Life Stream.*[10] *Masters are nothing but the waves of the ocean of the Lord. The relationship of the Master and the Lord is the relationship of the wave with the ocean.*[11] Furthermore, he comments: *All Masters are the same. They are all waves of the same ocean. The body is not the Master. Master is that Power, that Shabd, that Nam* [Word]. *Our real Master is that Shabd* [that Word]. . . *All Masters are one; there is no difference.*[12]

Because Masters are the *Word made flesh*, the *Shabd made flesh*, the *Sound Current made flesh*, the

Audible Life Stream made flesh, they are *God made flesh*
and, hence, are indestructible. *The Master never dies.*
He is Energy. He is Sound Current.[13]   In fact, God
Himself assumes the form of a Master and comes into
the world to lift poor souls out of the misery and pain
into which they have fallen. Through the link of the
Word, He joins the seeker to Himself and thus bestows
God Realization on the disciple.[14]

The Master, the Perfect Saint, the Sat Guru, is
omniscient.[15]   Saints know all about the past, present
and future.[16]   There is nothing they do not know. They
are waves of the ocean of the Lord. They are the
Essence of God Himself.

Saints set forth three basic postulates: 1. There is a
God. 2. Our soul is, in essence, a drop of the Ocean of
the Lord whence it separated so long ago as to have
totally forgotten its Divine Origin. 3. God is within us
and cannot be realized anywhere outside.[17]   Christ
emphatically corroborated this fundamental truth by
saying: *Behold, the Kingdom of God is within you* [St.
Luke 17:21]. Such is the message of all mystics and
Perfect Masters.

How does one recognize a Perfect Master, a true
Saint? Basically, through the following four principles:

1. Saints inculcate a realization of God *within* one's
self, not without one's self.

2. Saints teach only the practice of the Word, the
Logos, the Shabd with love and service to the Perfect

Messages from the Masters

Living Master of the time, just as Christ's followers rendered to him love and service.

3. Saints develop love for the Supreme Being by detaching seekers from their worldly attachments. This is why Christ said in St. Matthew 10:34: *Think not that I am come to send peace on earth: I came not to send peace, but a sword.* Why a sword? To sever his disciples from this world so they could journey *Within* to the Kingdom of God.

4. Saints, themselves, spend most of their time in Spiritual Practice and Devotion and insist their disciples do the same.[18]

Catalogue of Saints

The messages of Saints are all the same--age to age, culture to culture, language to language. They all extol the worship of the Lord and His Word. Their words may be different in order to accommodate peoples of the same language, but the concepts and principles are identical.

In this volume of *Messages from the Masters*, the overwhelming number of quotations come from nine Perfect Saints. As one will soon deduce, they all have the same messages although they may use slightly different words to convey them. Each, also, has his own distinctive personality and manner of delivery. We must remember that cultures are different, attitudes are different and historic times are different. For example, the manner and style of speaking three hundred years ago to people in India, Pakistan and that region of the world and in those cultures was different from other places and cultures in the world at the same time. Today's climate, cultures, mores, etc. are also different so one will see a variance in the type and style of language used. However, the messages, as the reader will see, are the same.

The nine featured Saints whose personal writings compose the majority of quotations in this text are:

1. Guru Ravidas
2. Kabir
3. Guru Nanak
4. Tulsi Sahib
5. Swami Ji Maharaj
6. Baba Jaimal Singh
7. Maharaj Sawan Singh Ji
8. Maharaj Jagat Singh Ji
9. Maharaj Charan Singh Ji

Following is a brief synopsis of each Saint. This is given to allow the reader an opportunity to become acquainted with each of these Perfect Masters who have given Spiritual Light to the world when they were in the world. In Chapter Three, *Masters: Part II* we will continue to delve more deeply into their teachings and discuss the advantages accruing to the soul through the association of a Perfect Saint.

Messages from the Masters

Guru Ravidas

Guru Ravidas, a Saint of the 15th and 16th Centuries, was born into a lowly cobbler's house on the outskirts of Banaras, India - a traditional stronghold of the priesthood. The dates of his birth and death are controversial. The three most prominent dates of his birth are: 1414, 1433 and 1434. His probable dates of death are: 1532, 1540 and 1552. Although specific life span dates also disagree, it has been mutually decided among scholars that Ravidas lived a long life, possibly 128 to 151 years.

A low-caste cobbler all his life, Guru Ravidas was regarded as one of the most distinguished Saints of his time and served as Master to kings, queens and men of importance. As many Mystics, he was not an academic scholar. His knowledge was based - as is that of all Perfect Masters - on his profound *inner experience.* Although all Masters teach the same spiritual truths, their personalities and styles of teaching vary. Guru Ravidas' presentation was in a spirit of gentle persuasion and humble submission.

All Saints also have Masters. Again, there is some controversy as to who Ravidas' Master was. It was either Kabir or Kabir's Master, Ramanand. Guru Nanak was also a contemporary of Ravidas. Thus, there were no less than three Perfect Masters alive on earth during this time. This is significant in as much as Saints tell us there is always at least one Perfect Saint on the earth at any given time for the purpose of escorting souls Home to God.

One of Ravidas' greatest and most famous disciples was Princess Mirabai, also known as Mira. She was of a royal class and is reputed to have been born in 1498. The earliest collection of the poems of Ravidas is available in the Sri Adi Granth which contains forty of his verses.

Other names for Guru Ravidas are: *Ramdas, Raidas, Rayidas, Ruidas, Ruhdas, Rohidas and Rudradas.*[19]

Kabir

Kabir, one of India's greatest Saints, was born in or about 1440, dying in 1518. Legend has it that Kabir was the result of an immaculate birth. As the tale goes, a Light descended from the sky at Lahar Talao near Banaras. Saint Ramanand, who was to become Kabir's Master, was told of this Light and he said it was the Light of a child who would be a great Saint. A poor Muslim weaver named Niru was walking with his wife Nima by the lake, spotted the child floating in the water and, since they did not have a child, considered taking it and raising it as their own. In their hesitance the child itself spoke and said that because of Nima's kindness to him in a previous life, he had come to rescue them from the Wheel of Transmigration and he wanted them to receive the merit of raising him, which they did.

Messages from the Masters

Kabir, meaning "Great; the greatness of God," spent his worldly life as a low-caste weaver. When his foster-father died when Kabir was ten or twelve, he applied his father's trade to support the household, but keeping the home fires burning was difficult because Kabir would often sit in meditation leaving the loom idle.

Kabir led a householder's life. Upon the death of his first wife, he married again. His second wife's name was Loi who was also raised by foster parents who found her wrapped in a blanket and floating on a river as well. They had two children, Kamal and Kamali.

Kabir, a Supreme Saint of the 15th and 16th Centuries was a contemporary of both Guru Ravidas and Guru Nanak, the latter to whom he was senior in age. His Master is widely held to be Ramanand but it is said that Kabir far surpassed his Master and was so great that, at a later stage, even Ramanand become Kabir's disciple.

Kabir's death was mystical. Just before he died he asked his attendants to leave his room. After he had passed, Muslim and Hindu followers disputed as to who should claim the body: the Muslims wanted to bury it; the Hindus cremate it, as designated by each of their respective religious traditions. When they entered his room to remove the shroud covering his body only a heap of flowers remained![20]

Guru Nanak

Born in 1469 *Guru Nanak* was also known as the Great Saint of the Punjab. He is believed to have been born in his father's house in a village called Talwandi Rai Bhoi, later known as Nankana Sahib, about forty miles from Lahore (now in Pakistan).

As a teenager, sometime between the ages of twelve and sixteen, he married Sulakhani, daughter of Mula. They had two sons: Sri Chand and Lakshmi Das. Because of his other-worldly interest and refusing to follow normal worldly activities such as herding buffalo, cultivating land, shop keeping and dealing in horses, Guru Nanak drove his father to despair. His family began to feel he had lost his reason for, as Nanak declares: *Some take me as one under an evil spell; others say that I am 'out of tune'. Some call me a man forsaken and woebegone; but I am mad after my Lord and I know of none but Him.* Eventually, however, Guru Nanak accepted a secular occupation as a storekeeper. He performed his duties by day but spent his nights engaged in meditation.

Guru Nanak, a contemporary of both Guru Ravidas and Kabir, is the first of the famous Ten Sikh Gurus. His writings compose part of the Granth Sahib (also known as the Adi Granth), an Eastern Indian Holy Text containing the writings of Saints. From his writings come such memorable quotes as: *How completely helpless mere men are; Remember the Lord, brothers -*

this is the way all must go, and *Ranks of this world will not be recognized in the next.*

Guru Nanak's departure from this world was much like Kabir's. As he lay dying, his Muslim and Hindu attendants each wanted his body to bury and cremate it respectively according to their normal practices. When Nanak pulled the sheets to his bed up over his head in preparation to depart this life, his followers paid their obeisance by bowing theirs. A few moments later they raised their heads, pulled the sheets back from his body to claim it but, presto! no Nanak. He relinquished his mortal frame at age seventy on 7 September 1539.[21]

Tulsi Sahib

Tulsi Sahib, whose birth name was Shyam Rao, was a Saint of the 19th Century. Born into a Brahmin family in 1763, he died in 1843 at the age of eighty. The eldest son of the King of Poona, young Shyam Rao was wed at an early age, against his own wishes, to a girl named Lakshmi Bai. From this union a son was born. Additionally, King Poona wanted to renounce his throne in favor of his son so he could spend the rest of his life in devotion. Tulsi Sahib, however, was averse to worldly pursuits, and the day before his ascension to his father's throne, he ran away from the palace, wandering in forests, mountains, towns and cities for many years, finally coming to settle in Hathras.

Although born into earthly noble ancestry in the royal lineage of the Peshwas, Tulsi Sahib renounced the world in order to attain spiritual realization. During his travels he even disguised himself to avoid recognition. Because he had come from the south, he was popularly known as *Dakhani Baba,* which means, "Sage from the South." His disciples called him 'Sahibji'.

Tulsi Sahib's works consist of: <u>Shabdavali</u>, <u>Ratan Sagar</u>, <u>Ghat Ramayan</u> and a small unfinished book called <u>Padma Sagar</u>. Of added interest is that Tulsi Sahib first used the expression "Sant Mat" [the *Teaching of Saints*] to stress the basic unity of the teachings of all Saints. Tulsi's most famous disciple was Shivdayal Singh who later came to be known as Swami Ji Maharaj, the renowned Saint and founder of the Radha Soami Faith.

Tulsi Sahib does not give the name of his Master in his writings but, nonetheless, ever espouses the absolute need of having a perfect Master. He says: *Without the guidance of a perfect Master, no one can ever get release from bondage, be he a god, man or sage. . . Without a Master, man will ever remain drifting in the dreadful ocean of the world.*

Tulsi Sahib, the Great Saint of Hathras, permanently lived in a hut in the small village of Jogia on the outskirts of Hathras. He lived there until he passed away in 1843 at the age of 80.[22]

Messages from the Masters

Swami Ji Maharaj

Swami Ji Maharaj was the Founder of the Radha Swami System of Philosophy and Spiritual Science. Swami Ji's real name was *Seth Shiv Dayal Singh.* He was born on 25 August 1818 in Agra, United Provinces, India. From an early age he began to expound the deepest spiritual truths. His Master was the Great Saint of Hathras, *Tulsi Sahib.*

After spending seventeen years in meditation in a dark, back room, Swami Ji began holding public satsang in January of 1861 at the age of forty-two. His teachings are embodied in two volumes of <u>Sar Barchan</u>: one in prose; one in poetry. Swami Ji Maharaj departed this earth plane on 15 June 1878, two months and ten days short of his sixtieth birthday.

The teachings of all Saints are the same and Swami Ji expounded the same truths as other Saints before him. The unique service rendered to mankind by Swami Ji, however, was the simple and lucid manner in which he taught the practice of the Sound Current, and thus brought its inestimable benefits within the reach of all humanity.

In doing this Swami Ji made all ancient Yoga systems outdated and unnecessary. The system of the Sound Current taught by Swami Ji brings to the devotee all the benefits ever accruing to the followers of the old system, doing it safely and much more speedily, carrying the student to spiritual heights never dreamed of by ancient Yogis. This was done by focusing the attention at the Third Eye or Tisra Til and moving upwards from there. This was the point at which most systems ended, thus being oblivious to the great realities laying deeper and infinitely higher Within.

As the Founder of the *Radha Swami [Soami] Science of the Soul*, elucidating the Teachings of the Saints, *Sant Mat*, Swami Ji became the patriarch of the current Radha Soami Divine Lineage of Saints, their order and number being:

1. Swami Ji Maharaj
2. Baba Jaimal Singh Ji
3. Maharaj Sawan Singh Ji
4. Maharaj Jagat Singh Ji
5. Maharaj Charan Singh Ji
6. Maharaj Gurinder Singh, i.e. 'Baba Ji'.[23]

Baba Jaimal Singh Ji

Baba Jaimal Singh was born in July of 1839. His father's name was Sardar Jodh Singh; his mother's, Shrimati Dayakaur. As with all Perfect Saints, his interest in spiritual matters began at an early age when, at seven years old, he read sacred writings of the Sikh Gurus and imbibed a great desire for spiritual practice, seeing some light inside even at that time.

While studying the *Granth Sahib* he learned of the Five Melodies reverberating within man, and when his closest spiritual friend, Baba Khem Das, could shed no light on the issue, Baba Ji began traveling about seeking light on this subject from various Mahatmas - great souls [highly spiritual persons]. However, none could help him.

He continued to search and search. Finally, his journey led him to a Perfect Mahatma in Agra. That Perfect Saint was Swami Ji. After a few discourses, Baba Jaimal Singh was initiated and, from that time on, spiritual practice was his main concern and. . . he made rapid progress. In fact, one day Swami Ji took his heir apparent disciple upward to the inner region of Daswan Dwar.

Baba Ji wanted to devote the great part of his time to devotional practice but Swami Ji counseled him that if he became a recluse he would be dependent on others for his sustenance and, therefore, advised him to earn his own livelihood. With that guidance, Baba Jaimal Singh enlisted in the army on the 14th of July 1857, specifically in the 24th Punjabis. It is said of him that he was often found sitting for spiritual practice the whole of the night. After thirty-four years of military service, Baba Ji retired on pension on the 18th of August, 1889.

He returned home for a short stay at Dhaliwal and came to Beas in 1891 and began to hold satsang (spiritual discourse; "Satsang" means 'true association') at age fifty-two. At this time the Dera (spiritual community in northern India) was little more than a small cabin squatting on the desert beneath the hot suns of summer and unsheltered from the chill winds of winter. Nonetheless, this was the beginning of the Dera which would later bear his name: Dera Baba Jaimal Singh, affectionately named by his successor, Maharaj Sawan Singh. Baba Ji passed from this earthly life on 29 December 1903, at the age of sixty-four.[24]

Maharaj Sawan Singh Ji

Ultimately to be known as *Great Master*, **Sawan Singh** was born on 27 July 1858, in the village of Mehmansing-walla in the district of Ludhiana, the Punjab, India. Forbidding any detailed or lengthy descriptions of himself, much of what is known must be omitted.

Great Master received collegiate training at Thomason Civil Engineering College, Roorkee, U.P. After college and after the death of his father, who had been a commissioned officer in the 14th Sikh Regiment, Sawan Singh followed his father's footsteps and joined the same regiment, retiring on pension in 1911 after twenty-eight years of military service.

Sawan Singh had long sought a real Master. He had studied Sikh scriptures and visited many Mahatmas in search of light. One day in the Murree Hills, Baba Jaimal Singh, then renowned for his spiritual holiness, told one of his disciples: "That is the man we have come to initiate," all of this, of course, unknown to Baba Ji's future successor. Sawan Singh heard of the holy man's

Messages from the Masters

presence and attended his satsangs. He was deeply interested in the teachings and on the 15th of October 1894 at age 36, Sawan Singh was initiated into the Radha Soami Faith. A short nine years later Baba Jaimal Singh turned over his work to Great Master in June of 1903.[25]

The spiritual colony of *Dera Baba Jaimal Singh*, lovingly named in his Master's memory, grew and flourished under Great Master's perfect guidance from the small cabin originally inhabited by Baba Jaimal Singh into a modern township. The Radha Soami Science grew also as Great Master initiated more than one hundred thousand people onto the spiritual path. Furthermore, the influence of Sant Mat expanded globally, reaching around the world to America, Europe, Africa, South America, Australia, New Zealand and beyond. For America, the year 1911 was spiritually auspicious because that was the year Sant Mat came to the United States. The first Americans to be initiated by Great Master were Dr. and Mrs. Brock of Port Angeles, Washington. Dr. Brock was the 2,250th initiate of Great Master, Maharaj Sawan Singh Ji.

Maharaj Sawan Singh Ji served as the revered leader of Sant Mat for 45 years from 1903 until his passing at age eighty-nine on 2 April 1948.[26]

Maharaj Jagat Singh Ji

Maharaj Jagat Singh Ji was born on 27 July 1884 at Nussi, a small village not very far from Beas. He received his education in the Mission School at Jullundur and later at the Government College, Lahore, where He took his M.Sc. degree in chemistry. Jagat Singh joined the Punjab Agricultural College in Lyallpur in 1911 as Assistant Professor of Chemistry. He retired as Vice-Principal of the institution in 1943.

When Jagat Singh was twenty-six years of age he was initiated into the Mystic Practice of Surat Shabd Yoga. This initiation occurred on 28 December 1910 and was given by Maharaj Sawan Singh Ji. Guru Ji, as he affectionately came to be known by staff and students, was extremely conscientious and assiduous in his spiritual devotion. His only two interests were his official duties and his spiritual practice. These he performed with unusual fervor. As with all true disciples, his faith in his Master, Maharaj Sawan Singh Ji, was steadfast and unshakable.

Upon his retirement in 1943, he spent practically all his time in meditation and spiritual practice. In April of 1948 at the age of sixty-four, Guru Ji assumed the Mastership of the Radha Soami Faith upon Great Master's passing. He served in this capacity for three and a half years until his transition at the age of sixty-seven on 23 October 1951.

Messages from the Masters

Because of his unique blend of being a scientist, professor and a practical Mystic, and therefore being able to satisfy both an intellectual and spiritual hunger, Guru Ji attracted quite a large following of intelligentsia in India as well as abroad. Unremitting in the discharge of his duties, he left the imprint of a masterly mind on whatever he undertook to do. He was a tower of strength, a strict disciplinarian whose sound judgment, humane methods and efficient handling of situations won him high esteem and honor.

Yet, Maharaj Jagat Singh was extremely tender at heart, self-effacing and unostentatious to an amazing degree. He talked little, used words sparingly, and went straight to the point, often quite bluntly. His life was exemplary and one of absolute detachment from all material cravings.[27]

Maharaj Charan Singh Ji

Maharaj Charan Singh was born into a respectable Sikh family of agriculturists[28] on the 12th of December 1916 at the home of his maternal grandparents in Moga, Punjab, India. His Master was his grandfather, Maharaj Sawan Singh Ji,[29] who initiated him into the Mystic Science of the Radha Soami Faith in 1933 when Charan was merely a teenager. [30]

Maharaj Charan Singh had two birth names: S. Charan Singh Grewal and S. Harbans Singh Grewal. From an early age he was placed in the care of his grandfather, Great Master, who guided, protected and molded him for the great leadership position of the Radha Soami Faith which Charan was destined to hold. At one point when he was approximately five years old, his grandfather directed him to meditate for a few minutes but young Charan exclaimed he did not want to because it was too bright inside! Such was the spiritually illumined state of this spiritually Divine child who would become the apotheosis of a Perfect Living Master!

Maharaj Charan Singh became a double graduate in Law and Arts and established a successful law practice. However, when Maharaj Jagat Singh passed on in October of 1951, naming Charan Singh as his successor, the thirty-four year old lawyer left his legal practice to assume the leadership role of the Radha Soami Faith headquartered at Dear Baba Jaimal Singh in the Punjab, India.

Maharaj Charan Singh Ji assumed the gaddi (mantle of leadership) on the 4th of November 1951--a day which he referred to as his execution - just five weeks shy of his thirty-fifth birthday. He held that spiritually esteemed position for nearly thirty-nine years until his physical withdrawal from the human frame on the 1st of June 1990 at 12:00 noon at the age of seventy-three.

During his Mastership of over thirty-eight years, Sant Mat - the Teachings of the Saints - flourished tremendously worldwide. Of the over 1,200,000 souls whom Maharaj Charan Singh Ji initiated into the Mystic Way, his first initiate was an American lady named Mrs. Kinzinger on 10 April 1953. He was the fifth Perfect Saint in the Radha Soami line of Perfect Living Masters.[31]

Notes

As one can see from the preceding sketches of the Saints whose quotes predominate the remainder of this text, many of them had to struggle through hardship to find their own Master in order to gain the spiritual connection their soul and destiny required for fulfillment. It is said that *every Saint has a past and every sinner has a future*, and by studying the lives of Perfect Masters we can be comforted that they understand our plight because they, too, had to live and experience struggle, which can be considered the prominent descriptive by-word for not only this world but for the spiritual path as well.

Additionally, these Perfect Masters held varying positions in the socio-economic framework of the world. Ravidas and Kabir lived lives which were rather low on the economic scale: Ravidas as a cobbler and Kabir as a weaver. On the other hand, Guru Nanak spent his worldly life as a storekeeper, while Tulsi Sahib was born of earthly royal ancestry. Baba Jaimal Singh and his successor, Maharaj Sawan Singh, both served in the military, while Jagat Singh was a college professor and Maharaj Charan Singh a lawyer. This demonstrates that following the Spiritual Path is not an activity of running away to the mountains, forests or deserts to find God. We can find him here and now in our very human bodies, in our very human lives and worldly occupations. Masters did it, and they preach and teach that it is the practical and natural way.

One crystalline clear thread of commonalty, however, of all these Saints, as their quotes express and testify, is that of their unadulterated love and devotion for the Lord as manifested through their own Master - their own Divine nexus or connective link with God. Their amalgamated, collective, clarion call to worship the Lord now in this human form by living a pure, spiritual life and attending to the spiritual work of meditation rings through the corridors of all ages, times, races, places, economic classes, countries, nations and peoples. Their great Message, their One Message, is that God is real and man can merge in Him while living in this very body by living a spiritual life under the guidance and protection of a Perfect Living Master.

Child of the Light

© Richard Andrew King

You are a Child of the Light,
a coruscating spire of white-fire flame,
a vortex of white-fire sun;
a crystalline spray of white-fire ray,
a soul whose time has come.
The universe beckons and God demands
you radiate your Light through space,
fusing your power this very hour,
illuminating the magnificence of your race,
a race where man is all in one,
non-separate and complete,
a single soul, in total, whole,
with multiple hands and feet.
Souls emerge and now converge
in a world approaching Dawn.
In inner space they see a race
where splendor flows in song;
where white-fire light inspires
and radiates the cosmic core,
where Beings rise in azure skies
to live forevermore.
Yes, you are a Child of the Light,
a coruscating spire of white-fire flame,
a vortex of white-fire sun,
a crystalline spray of white-fire ray,

a soul whose time has come.

So cast white-fire higher;

let consciousness rise to see;

let soul explore the secret door

that leads to infinity.

The time is now. The space is here.

Excuse yourself no more.

Radiate Light, extinguish night

and live forevermore.

For you are a Child of the Light,

a coruscating spire of white-fire flame,

a vortex of white-fire sun,

a crystalline spray of white-fire ray,

a soul whose time has come.

Bibliography: Chapter Two

1   *Guru Nanak, His Mystic Teachings*, J. R. Puri, Radha Soami Satsang Beas, Punjab, India, 1982 p. 91

2   *Spiritual Gems*, Maharaj Sawan Singh Ji, Radha Soami Satsang Beas, Punjab, India, 1965, L 103

3   *The Master Answers*, Maharaj Charan Singh Ji, Radha Soami Satsang Beas, Punjab, India, 1966, A 407

4   Ibid., A 211

5   *Guru Nanak*, pp. 94-95

6   *The Master Answers*, A. 13

7   Ibid., A 21

8   *Kabir The Great Mystic*, Isaac A Ezekiel, Radha Soami Satsang Beas, 4th edition, Punjab, India, 1979, p. 162

9   *Spiritual Gems*, L 195

10   *The Master Answers*, A 31

11   Ibid., A 36

12   Ibid., A 241

13   *The Science of the Soul*, Maharaj Sardar Bahadur Jagat Singh, RSSB, 5th edition, 1977, p. 167

14   Ibid., p. 11

15   *Sar Bachan*, Swami Ji Maharaj, Radha Soami Satsang Beas, Punjab, India, 5th edition, 1971, # 117

16   *Spiritual Gems*, L 157

17   *The Science of the Soul*, p. 2

18   *Sar Bachan*, # 40

19   *Guru Ravidas: Life and Teachings*, K.N. Upadhyaya, Radha Soami Satsang Beas, Punjab, India, 1982, pp. 3-21

20   *Kabir The Great Mystic*, Isaac A Ezekiel, Radha Soami Satsang Beas, 4th edition, Punjab, India, 1979, pp. 7-21

21   *Guru Nanak, His Mystic Teachings*, J. R. Puri, Radha Soami Satsang Beas, Punjab, India, 1982 pp. 3-40,

22   *Tulsi Sahib, Saint of Hathras*, J.R. Puri/V.K. Sethi, Radha Soami Satsang Beas, 1981 pp. 1-19

23   *Sar Bachan*, Swami Ji Maharaj, Radha Soami Satsang Beas, Punjab, India, 5th edition, 1971, pp. 2-3

24   Ibid., pp. 3-6

25   Ibid., pp. 6-7

26   *The Dawn of Light*, Maharaj Sawan Singh Ji, RSSB, Punjab, India, 1985, cover to p. 7

27   *The Science of the Soul*, Maharaj Sardar Bahadur Jagat Singh, RSSB, 5th edition, 1977, forward

28   *Divine Light*, Maharaj Charan Singh, RSSB, Punjab, India, 4th edition, 1976, cover

29   *The Dawn of Light*, Maharaj Sawan Singh, RSSB, 1985, p. 19

30   *Divine Light*, cover

31   *Treasure Beyond Measure*, Shanti Sethi, RSSB, 2nd edition, 1991

Chapter Three

MASTERS: PART II

God, Guru and Saint are the same in consciousness.
This is the eternal, essential truth of the scriptures.
Make no distinction among them.[1]

As we recall from *Masters: Part I*, Masters - also known as Perfect Saints and Gurus (with initial capital letters designating their divine quality) - are manifestations of God on earth. They are the *Word made flesh* and they are One with God. In fact, there is no distinction between the Master, the Saint, the Guru and God. As Guru Ravidas declares: *God, Guru and Saint are the same in consciousness. This is the eternal, essential truth of the scriptures. Make no distinction among them.*

Saints come to save souls from the world, not save the world. Their mission is to detach, cut and sever the ties that bind the soul to this creation and reattach it to the Creation of the Lord. Contrary to popular belief, they are not concerned in the least with making the world a paradise nor a better place in which to live. As Christ said in St. Matthew 10:34: *Think not that I am come to send peace on earth: I came not to send peace, but a sword.*

A sword. A sword! A sword is what Christ came to send unto the world! How strange that his very message of bringing a sword to sever souls from their extreme attachment to this place of darkness so they could go Home to God should be precisely inverted by many people who preach that his message was to bring peace on earth. Christ knew, as all Saints know, that this is God's creation and God has not willed this earth to be a paradise but a proving ground for the soul, a prison house in which the soul is continually incarnated and incarcerated in multitudes of living forms throughout eons of time until it has had enough with the illusion and nonsense of living in and being saturated by external phenomena in this nefarious and ephemeral world and thereby totally reverses and redirects its consciousness to becoming God-focused, God-realized and returning Home to the Lord Himself.

But to return to God, we must *love* God, we must be drenched and dripping with devotion to God. But how can we love God? As Christ says in St. John 6:46: *Not that any man hath seen the Father, save he which is of God, he hath seen the Father.*

All of us normal mortals have never seen God. As Christ also says in St. John 4:24: *God is a Spirit, and they that worship him must worship him in spirit and in truth.* Mere mortals cannot *see* Spirit, which is why Christ said that no man has ever seen God. And God knows this. So what does He do? He manifests Himself in the form of a Perfect Living Master who can be seen by mere mortals, mere men; who can, therefore, have a *Living Essence* and *Presence* of God with which to identify, with which to love. By loving a Living Master and obeying his commands, by following him in action, not words, we are, in fact, loving God. We now have the numinous nexus, the spiritual connection we obligatorily need, to return Home to the Lord.

Thus, what we cannot see, we cannot love, but what we can see, we can love. Enter the Perfect Saint. As Professor J. R. Puri states: *The Master is the manifest form of the Lord, and it is the manifest form that can be the object of love. And if God can only be realized through love, the Master is an indispensable link for God-realization.*[2]

Thus, Saint Ravidas, in praise of his own Master and in praise of all Masters says: *Grant me, O God of gods, the company of the Saint, a taste for the Saint's discourses and love for the Saint. Bless me with the Saint's conduct, the Saint's way. He alone is wise, O Ravidas, who knoweth that no difference is there between the Saint and God.*[3]

What does Ravidas ask for? The *company, taste for the messages, love for* and *conduct of* the Saint. It is not enough simply to hear a Message from a Master. We need to have his company, love and conduct, conduct expressed through our own personal behavior. In other words, listening to sermons will not get us to Paradise. We must find a Saint, dwell in his company, love him, love his discourses and, this is the critical aspect, conduct ourselves like him. In other words, *live* a purely spiritual life - not simply talk about a spiritual life.

This is the crux of Christ's words when he said in St. John 14:15: *If you love me, keep my commandments.* Don't just listen to me talk, listen to me speak, become enthralled with my miracles, make up your own version of what I'm telling you. Do what I am directing you to do. That's how you truly love me and that's how I recognize your love. *Conduct* your selves like I conduct myself. If you listen to my words but behave differently, it is clearly indicative that you do not really love me, that you do not really care for me or my teachings. In fact, it is clearly indicative of your hypocrisy, of saying one thing and doing another.

And so it is with each of us in regard to Saints in general and our Master, if we have one, in specific. To love a Master is to follow his teachings and to conduct ourselves accordingly. This is why Guru Ravidas unequivocally declares: *Bless me with the Saint's conduct, the Saint's way.*

The Master, the Satguru, is the *One who gives Light.*[4] *Satguru Himself is the Lord incarnate and to*

Messages from the Masters

serve Him is to serve the Lord. Those who try to realize the Supreme Being but ignore the Sat Guru will never find Him. But those who are in the service of a Sat Guru have already found the Lord and when their eyes are opened, they will recognize Him.[5]

But how do we reconcile the apparent form of a man, which the Master ostensibly is, with that of him being God, the Lord incarnate? Guru Nanak tells us: *The difference between the Perfect Mystic and God is that while the former exists in the human body and on the physical plane, the latter exists in His Absolute, Transcendent State.*[6] At man's level of normal, human, uninitiated consciousness in this material realm, he simply is incapable of reaching that realm where he can know God as Saints know Him because they come from His highest realm. When man becomes Initiated into the Mystic Way and onto the Spiritual Path by a Perfect Saint, then he will be able to eventually *know* God by *direct experience*, not by philosophy or intellect.

Past vs. Living Masters

And what about past masters? Can they not help us spiritually? Certainly their teachings can inspire us and give us a code to live by but, unfortunately, no more. Nanak points out that past masters *cannot take us to the transcendent regions now, nor can they give us any guidance in our spiritual journey within.*[7] For God-realization we need a *Living* Master, a *Living* Son of

God to impart God's *Living Word* - His Logos, His *Celestial Music*, His *Audible Life Stream*. We need a Perfect *Living* Master to plug us in to the *Living* Current of God. A past master is analogous to a drawing or photograph of light. We see the image of light in the drawing or photo but the light is not real. It is emitting no real energy. On the other hand, a real light bulb drawing power from an active *live* source of energy radiates *live, living energy, living light.* So it is with past and current Masters. Past Masters are only images of light. Living Masters are *Living Light.*

As Maharaj Charan Singh comments: *Saints of the past cannot help us no matter how great they were in their lifetime. Only the Saint whom we have met in our lifetime and who takes us under his protection can help us at the time of death.*[8] *The Masters and Saints of the past have finished their work in this world and have merged back into the Father.*[9] *In short,* says Tulsi Sahib, *it is impossible for anyone to attain salvation by simply believing in or worshipping a Saint, prophet, incarnation or god who lived in the past.*[10] This is corroborated by Isaac Ezekiel who states: *Those who are serious in their search for God must go to a contemporary Perfect Master. . . Past Masters cannot give us salvation.*[11]

But not to fear. As discussed in *Masters: Part I*, the world has never been nor will ever be without a Perfect Living Master. There simply *can be no single savior for*

Messages from the Masters

the whole world for all times and until the end of time.[12] When the disciple is ready, the Master will appear. Says Charan Singh: *Every Saint is sent into this world for particular souls - allotted souls, and those souls will come to him. They alone will have faith in him. They alone will be receptive to his teachings. They alone will practice meditation and go back to the Father.*[13] All of this will happen as naturally as leaves fall from a tree. There is no need to worry. When the time is right and at the precisely ordained time according to one's karmas, one will meet the Master.

Maharaj Charan Singh reassures us: *If anyone is sincere and honest in his devotion and really wants to worship the true Lord, then the onus is on the Lord Himself to put him on the path. That person will ultimately come to a living Master, get initiation and follow the path to God-Realization.*[14] But we must be sincere.

He continues: *Merely saying that you worship God does not entitle you to become His disciple or His devotee.*[15] Here, of course, the Master is pointing out that our desire to meet the Lord must be unequivocally genuine. But there is another caveat. The Lord must *accept us*. In truth, the Master must accept us. We cannot merely accept him. It is a two-way transaction. Charan Singh says: *You have to be accepted by a living Master and then follow the path back to Him* [God).

Then, stage by stage, mansion by mansion, you will reach the ultimate destination.[16]

But before we ask to be accepted by the Master, Charan Singh says: *We must make a thorough research before we submit ourselves to any Master. Even if our whole life is spent in making investigation, making a research, it is not time lost, it is time gained. We are building on a very deep foundation, we are building on a rock. . . And if we are sincere, I assure you, He* [God] *puts us on the right Path. He does guide us.*[17] *What we need is a real yearning and devotion for Him. Then it is His responsibility to work out how to put us on the Path.*[18] *Those who really want, they always seek, they always find. And those who do not want, they do not seek*[19] and, obviously, do not find.

But then, again, he says: *It is not by coincidence that we come to the Path or to a Master. We are led in that direction. Though we may think it is coincidence, it is the effect of our karmas that we are automatically led to the Path. Wherever we may be born, ultimately our karma will bring us to the Path when that time comes. Actually, one who is to come to the Path is being guided right from the beginning.*[20] In effect, *each seeker is being driven to the Path according to his own karma.*[21]

But this is not so easy. As Kabir says: *Devotion to the Name of the Lord with genuine love is very rare; yea, very, very rare.*[22] Furthermore, it will be easy to differentiate those who are spiritually devoted and those

Messages from the Masters

who are not. As Swami Ji states: *Those who are ready to receive the teachings of the Saints will accept them; but those who are not ready will simply discuss and argue.*[23]   The bottom line, says Swami Ji, is that *one with great good fortune will surely meet a Sant Sat Guru,*[24] the Supreme Spiritual Mystic. *Sat Guru Himself is the Lord incarnate and to serve Him is to serve the Lord. Those who try to realize the Supreme Being but ignore the Sat Guru will never find Him. But those who are in the service of a Sat Guru have already found the Lord and when their eyes are opened, they will recognize Him.*[25]

This is also corroborated by Guru Nanak. *One meets with Saints*, says Nanak, *if one is blessed with perfect good fortune. They are the Lord's own, they dwell in the bliss of Truth. They surrender to the Lord spontaneously their mind and body.*[26] *He who serves the Guru knows the Lord; his sorrows depart and through the Word he realizes the Truth.*[27]

Getting to this point of meeting with a Saint is no easy task. As Maharaj Sawan Singh Ji declares: *Purity of character is the fundamental basis on which the edifice of spiritual progress is to be built.*[28] *Character is the foundation upon which rises the spiritual edifice. As long as one is a slave of the senses, talk of spirituality is a mockery . . . The first essential step to a spiritual life is character. One may deceive one's friends, relatives and even oneself, but the Power Within is not deceived.*[29]

It is quite clear what Saints are saying. If we want to worship God, we must first love God. He must be the driving force of our desires, needs and wants. But since we can't see Him because He is a Spirit - and it's hard to love what we cannot see - He manifests Himself in a form which we can see and with which we can identify, i.e. the Perfect Living Master, the Saint, the Sant Sat Guru who is the Lord incarnate. The Master is *the* Son of God, the wave of the ocean of God. He is the *Word, Logos, Shabd, Sound Current, Audible Life Stream,* made flesh. By loving Him, we love God because God's true essence is manifested by and radiates from his very being, the being in which God chose to manifest Himself and make Himself known to the world.

The Master, however, must be a Perfect *Living* Master. Past Masters cannot help us achieve salvation because they cannot connect us to the *Living* Word, the *Living* Sound Current, the *Living* Audible Life Stream (see *The Word*). It's very axiomatic. Past Masters are dead. The *Current* Master is alive. That which is dead cannot connect us to that which is alive. A picture of light is not light. It is only an image of light. It is really dead light. It has absolutely no reality. It Radiates no *actual* light and dispels no darkness. Put a picture of light in a dark room and the room remains dark. Put a light bulb in a dark room, connect it to a living source of energy - a live electric current - turn it on, and, walah! *real* light instantly streams forth, radiating actual light

Messages from the Masters

and dispelling the darkness in the room. So it is with a *Living Master*. He is the *living source of spiritual energy* that connects us to God, dispels our spiritual darkness and centers us in the Light, and it is impossible to be a *living light* ourselves if we are not connected to a *live, living source of energy*.

Masters assure us that if we want to be that *living light* we can be. We simply have to find the *Living Light Source*, the Master, and connect with him. And we don't have to be concerned about not finding him because God has so ordained that this world will never be without at least one Perfect Living Master at all times. If we are *genuinely* sincere in meeting the Lord, He will, in fact, put us in contact with the Living Master. We do not have to worry about not finding him. He will find us and draw us to him.

However, when we find him *he* must *accept* us. We can't simply accept him and think we have a Master and we are his disciple. Our relationship with him is a two-way street. We cannot simply accept him and believe we are involved in a true relationship. The basic nature of any relationship is that there must be two parties and there must be a *mutual* agreement of consent between the parties involved. Otherwise, no real relationship exists.

Furthermore, if we meet a Living Master, Saints tell us that such a meeting is *not* coincidental. Any one who meets a Saint was destined to meet him right from the

66

very beginning. Nothing happens by chance in this creation. There are absolutely no accidents. All is a result of karma, and it is the result of great good karma that we do, in fact, meet a Perfect Master. As Guru Nanak says: *One meets with Saints if one is blessed with perfect good fortune.*

But. . . when we meet him, we will have done so by harboring a strong desire to love the Lord. In the Master's presence and under his guidance we will have to lead a pure life and exude purity of character, for *purity of character*, says Maharaj Sawan Singh, *is the fundamental basis on which the edifice of spiritual progress is to be built*, and it simply cannot be built without it. Actions, not mere words, are the hallmark of a true disciple of a Living Master. Talk is cheap. . . and empty. Actions do our real talking and exhibit our true intent and motive. God cannot be fooled. Nor can His Sons. To maintain our relationship with the Master we must be pure in thought and action and follow his teachings, do what he commands. Love is expressed through obedience. As every Master directs his disciples: *if you love me, keep my commandments.*

In *Masters: Part I* we learned how to recognize a Master, but how will we recognize a Master who is meant for us personally? Corroboration will come from within. Everything comes from within. *He* will pull us. *He* will make us know. We will have no doubts that we are meant for him and he is meant for us. The Master knows his flock and the sheep know their Master.

The Keeper of the Keys

As Christ tells us in St. Luke: 17:21: *The Kingdom of God is within you.* So it is. But none of us can find it without the numinous nexus - the divine, spiritual connection - which *is* the Perfect Master. He, and only he, *is* the *keeper of the keys to the Kingdom of God.*

As we read Jesus Christ's words in St. John: 14:6: *I am the way, the truth and the life: no man cometh unto the Father but by me*, he is saying that he, Christ, is the *keeper of the keys to the Kingdom of God.* But what he means is that 'I the master', not the personality Jesus, 'am the keeper of the keys'. 'I the master' am the one ordained by God to collect those lost sheep whom God wanted returned to Him at that time.

Furthermore, we know that Christ could not possibly have been insinuating that he was the only Master for all time. He says quite clearly, irrefutably and incontestably in St. John 9:5: *As long as I am in the world, I am the light of the world. As long as I am in the world*, he says, not 'for as long as the world exists'. He was very specific. In other words, the time period for his Mastership carried with it a specific, certain, definite time span. That time frame for him being *the light of the world* was limited to the duration of his life span and no longer--*for as long as I am in the world*, <u>he</u> said. Christ knew he had a set time frame for his Mastership and he taught this. All Masters teach the same. They are the light of the world as long as they are in the world because, through them, God shares His *Living*, not dead, *Word*; His *Living*, not dead, energy: His *Living*, not dead, light. But no Master is the light of the world for all time. They all corroborate this.

However, *as long as they are in the world* all Saints are *the light of the world.* They are the *keepers of the keys to the Kingdom of God.* Without them, we can knock all we want on His Door but we will not be able to gain entrance within. As Maharaj Charan Singh says: *Every Master tells us that we must go to a living Master. It is only through the path given to us by a living Master that we can go back to the Father. This is clearly stated in all scriptures including the Bible.*[30] *Even a Master,* he says, *needs a Master before he actually becomes a Master. Everyone who wants to go back to the Father needs a living Master, for if we could go back by our own efforts, there would never have been a need for Christ or any of the Redeemers to come into this world.*[31]

This is corroborated by Sawan Singh: *A living teacher is needed to school our children; a living doctor to prescribe for our ailments; a living judge to settle our disputes, and a living Master to give us our lost Jewel - the Word.*[32] The *Word*, of course, is the *Audible Life Stream,* the *Sound Current,* the *Shabd* and *Nad.* Huzur

Swami Ji Maharaj offers this direct fact: *The Lord and the Guru are one and there is no difference between them. You will not realize the Lord by worshipping Him directly but, by worshipping and serving the Sat Guru, you will realize God. The Lord Himself has ordained that He can be realized only through the Guru* (the Perfect Saint, the Living Master). *One without a Guru will have no access to His Kingdom. But the Guru must be a perfect one.*[33]

He continues: *Real knowledge of the Lord can be obtained only with the help of a perfect Sat Guru and it is imperative that the seeker should find such a Sat Guru. . . Those who are content with only the teachings of departed Saints are not true seekers and shall not see Him.*[34] As mentioned earlier, *it is impossible for anyone to attain salvation by simply believing in or worshipping a Saint. . . who lived in the past.*[34]

Tulsi Sahib shares his thoughts in this manner: *Without the guidance of a Perfect Master, no one can ever get release from bondage, be he a god, man or sage. . . Without a Master man will ever remain drifting in the dreadful ocean of the world.*[35] And, he adds: *The unsolvable mystery is solved by the Master alone. He shows the path to the inaccessible and the way to hit the target.*[36]

Of his own Master, this *Great Saint of Hathras* comments: *My Master has given to me knowledge of the self. Time and again my soul ascends to celestial regions. Traversing the regions within, I beheld the Cosmos* (physical, astral and causal regions). *The beginning and the end of Time stand revealed to me.*[37]

Guru Nanak declares: *Without the intercession of a perfect Master, a Satguru, no one will realize God.*[38] And further: *Without the guidance of the true guru, we cannot find the Name* (the Word, Logos, Sound Current, Shabd, Nad). *Without the Name life has no purpose. It is birth and death and regret. It is like the crow visiting a deserted house.*[39] And, in praise of his Master, he remarks: *I have no sanctuary save His Name. It is my only treasure. My Guru gave it to me. I am forever beholden to Him.*[40]

The cobbler Saint, Guru Ravidas, asserts: *Guru is the Grand Philosopher's Stone. . . The Satguru hath shown me the way. Sins of past lives were destroyed and all my agonies came to an end. Unstruck Divine Music sounded within and the inaccessible wisdom was attained by the grace of the Master.*[41]

Now, Guru Ravidas was no light-weight Saint. He was a Perfect Master. But he, like all Saints, extols the merits of having a personal Master and expresses boundless gratitude and love for him. But what is the *unstruck music sounded within* referred to by Ravidas? Why does he use the word *inaccessible* in referring to wisdom? And, what was *the way* his Satguru had shown him? A major clue is found in Christ's statement: *The light of the body is the eye; therefore, when thine eye is single, thy whole body also is full of light.* [St. Luke: 11:37)

Are Saints the only ones who speak of the unstruck melody, the sound current, the audible life stream? Dr. Albert Einstein, the world's foremost scientist of the 20th Century and Nobel Laureate states:

> *Everything is determined, the beginning as well as*
> *the end by forces over which we have no control. It*
> *is determined for the insect as well as for the star.*
> *Human beings, vegetables or cosmic dust, we all*
> *dance to a mysterious tune intoned in the distance*
> *by an invisible piper?*

This is an incredible statement made, not by a Saint, but by a scientist. What is the *mysterious tune* of which Einstein speaks? And what is the *invisible piper*? Obviously, Einstein's world of science discovered something mystical, some *mysterious tune* intoned by an *invisible piper*, beyond the walls and halls of itself. Einstein also said this:

> *Everyone who is seriously involved in the pursuit of*
> *science becomes convinced that a spirit is manifest*
> *in the laws of the universe, a spirit vastly superior*
> *to that of man and one in the face of which we, with*
> *our modest powers, must feel humble.*

When not only Saints speak of the sound current but the most eminent scientist of his time does as well, would it not behoove us to also investigate this reality? Would our spiritual ascent not be benefited by such profound statements? Saints know it. Einstein knew it. So can we.

The Tenth Door

Saints refer to the human body as having ten doors. Nine open *out*; one opens *in*. The nine outward-opening doors are the openings through which man connects with the world and remains attached, nay, chained to it. The tenth inward-opening door is the opening through which man connects with the Kingdom of God and journeys through it back to his Home with the Lord.

The nine doors are the physical orifices of the human body: the two eyes, the two ears, the two nostrils, the mouth and the two lower apertures of procreation and elimination. Through these *doors* our vital energy and consciousness flow outward and downward into the world connecting us with it, enslaving us to it, engulfing us in its illusion, deception and incarcerating darkness.

However, the *Tenth Door* is the *Mystic Door*. Unlike the other nine, it opens *inward* and takes the soul *upward* to the regions of resplendent light, to the inner spiritual realms of God's higher worlds. This *Tenth Door* in mystic language is also called the *Third Eye*. When, with the help of the Master - the Keeper of the Keys to the Kingdom of God - this *eye* is opened, the soul perceives the light of God within. Thus, when Christ says: *The light of the body is the eye; therefore, when thine eye is single, thy whole body also is full of light*, he is directly referring to the opening of the *Tenth Door*, the *Third Eye* (singular), the only door of the human body which opens *inward*, the door which *is* the secret passageway to the Lord's inner mansions.

This *Tenth Door*, this *Third Eye*, is located slightly above and midway between the two eyebrows in the human body. It is not present in any other living form. This *Eye* is where one 'knocks' to enter into God's Kingdom. As Christ said in St. Matthew 7:7: *Knock and it shall be opened unto you.* In other words, this *Tenth Door*, this *Eye*, becomes the focal point of one's meditation, one's incessant petition to the Lord by calling His *Name* and listening to His *Word.*

Guru Nanak comments on this Tenth Door: *Unlike the bodies of the lower animals, the human body is not confined to the nine outlets. It has a secret tenth door which is the gateway to the Lord. This can be opened only through instruction from a living Master who imparts the technique of achieving it. The company of such a teacher. . . is indispensable. . . for the Guru has himself traversed the path and is a necessary guide for saving the disciple from many dangerous pitfalls.*[42]

Here we see the major benefit of the Master's company. He alone can open this *Tenth Door,* this secret passageway. No mere mortal can do it. Normal mortals do not even know of this door and even if they did, they are helpless to open it. For this, one needs a Master. It is obligatory. The Master *is*, therefore, as we can clearly see, the *Keeper of the Keys to the Kingdom of God.*

Furthermore, if we want to gain entrance to God's Kingdom by going through this *Tenth Door*, through this *secret passageway* where *thy body shall be full of light*, we must find a Perfect Living Master and seek Initiation from Him. We must please him. We must be worthy of him. If we do not and are not, true salvation is simply impossible. Says Swami Ji Maharaj: *Be it known that the Inner Secret is known only to a Sant Sat Guru or to one to whom He has revealed it.*[43]

Rescue of the Soul

Why do we need a Master in the first place? Isn't it wonderful to be a human being living and experiencing the world, soaking it all up, indulging in its many and varied pleasures, living in the moment, going for the gusto; *eating, drinking and being merry for tomorrow we may die*? We only live once, right? Wrong.

Life is a continuum of life. . . and death. Saints inform us that there are 8,400,000 living forms into which the soul can incarnate, and that the human form is the only one in which it can realize God (see *Reincarnation*). If we lose the opportunity of this human form by squandering it in sensual and worldly pursuits, we may never get it again and never getting it again, we will never have the opportunity of returning Home to the Lord and ending our slavery.

Messages from the Masters

From the time God sent us into this creation we have been transmigrating this Wheel of forms for millions of years, eons of time, living in one body and then another. Now, however, we are inhabiting the *human form* and we have a chance of escape (see *The Human Form*). It is the Perfect Living Master who rescues us from this Wheel of Transmigration, takes us out of this creation and returns us to our true Home in the Royal Realm of the Lord God Almighty.

Maharaj Charan Singh Ji comments: *Our Master is the only one who is competent to take us back to the Father so that we may get everlasting life and never have to come back to this world at all. Through his help we will be rescued from the condemnation of birth and death - the transmigration of the soul. As it is now, before we are on the path, we hardly get rid of one body before we become the victim of another birth according to our past deeds. Sometimes, in between, there is also a period of time in which we reap reward in heaven or suffer in hell before being sent back into this world. But as soon as we are on the path, under the guidance of a Living Master, we are on our way to eternal liberation and salvation. As long as we are away from the Father and not on the path leading back to Him, we are all condemned. To pass from death unto life, therefore, means that while everybody has to face death, those who are on the path will never have to die again because they will never be born again. They alone will get everlasting life after this death.*[44]

Condemned. That's what we are without a Perfect Master - condemned to an existence of suffering within the Wheel of Transmigration, constantly being born and dying again, again and again. Condemned. It is not a pleasant thought.

Thus, as we live in this human form we have a choice: lead a spiritual life and follow a Saint, or experience the dreadful Wheel of Transmigration after our human life ends and remain in this dark dimension for untold and insufferable eons. When confronted with such a choice, there really is no choice. Any clear thinking, sentient, spiritually-focused soul can only scream for rescue by a Perfect Master when confronted with the reality of remaining in this dimension of darkness for an interminable period of time. And, as Maharaj Charan Singh declares of those who are on the spiritual path, *They alone will get everlasting life after this death.* That means that those who are not on the spiritual path, will not gain everlasting life.

Summary

Masters are the Lord Incarnate. Their mission is to free people from this world and take them Home to the Lord by connecting each individual soul to its Source through the *Word* of God, the *Audible Life Steam,* the *Sound Current,* the *Shabd, Nam* and *Nad.* They teach

Messages from the Masters

pure spirituality. They have no desire to save the world. Their only desire is to save souls *from* the world.

Saints come in all climes, speak in all tongues, inhabit every race, culture, economic status and profession. The world has never been without Saints, nor will it ever be. God has so ordained that at least one of His Sons be present on the earth at all times to shed enlightenment, to be *the light of the world* and to rescue souls from its clutches as well as the clutches of the Wheel of Transmigration.

For the soul to return Home to God, it must love God or at least have a longing to return to Him. *Without the company of Saints, Divine love cannot arise; and without love, devotion to the Lord is impossible.*[45] But, *he who remembereth God's Name, having sought the company of a Saint, his miseries are averted.*[46]

As Kabir proclaims: *The Master's authority reigns supreme over the head of all. Not a shadow of doubt remains on this point.*[47] To be spiritually evolved, one must seek a Master. There is no other option.

As Guru Nanak reminds us: *Let no one remain in delusion in the world; without the Guru no one shall ever go across the ocean of phenomena.*[48] *A true Guru is one who has in his spiritual transport realized the Ultimate Reality and who enables others to attain that Reality.*[49] *God and his Mystics are one; take them not as different due to their human form. As the wave riseth above the water and mergeth into it again, so do Saints merge into the Lord.*[50] *The true Guru, in his mercy, ministers to us the Truth. He dispels all one's woes and puts one on the Path. Yea, no thorn pricks the foot of one whom the true Guru protects and redeems.*[51] *The true Guru knows the secrets of the inner realms and it is through the Guru's Word that one realizes the fearless One. Looking within thyself, find thy Lord and stray thou not elsewhere.*[52]

Master's Work

© Richard Andrew King

The Master's work is Perfect,

more perfect than we know;

and what we see is dazzling

in body, mind and soul.

No architect, however schooled,

could be more perfect than the Lord;

only through experience

can one corroborate His Word.

As we come to learn, whatever is,

is Perfect by His Hand.

We may not like or care for it,

but we will understand

that His ways and means have purpose--

to edify the soul,

to cleanse and purify us

and make our beings whole.

It is a wonderment to see

Perfection manifest in awe;

surely we will know His Grace

in obeisance to His Law.

Bibliography: Chapter Three

1   Guru Ravidas: Life and Teachings, K.N. Upadhyaya, Radha Soami Satsang Beas, Punjab, India, 1982, p. 64

2   Guru Nanak: His Mystic Teachings, J.R. Puri, Radha Soami Satsang Beas, Punjab, India, 1982, p. 91

3   Guru Ravidas, pp. 113-114

4   Kabir The Great Mystic, Isaac A. Ezekiel, Radha Soami Satsang Beas, Punjab, India, 4th edition, p. 229

5   Sar Bachan, Huzur Swami Ji Maharaj, Radha Soami Satsang Beas, Punjab, India, # 142

6   Guru Nanak, p. 92

7   Ibid., p. 92

8   St. John: The Great Mystic, Maharaj Charan Singh Ji, RSSB, Punjab, India, p. 55

9   Ibid., p. 89

10   Sar Bachan, # 52

11   Kabir The Great Mystic, p. 250

12   Ibid., p. 155

13   The Master Answers, Maharaj Charan Singh Ji, RSSB, Punjab, India, 1966, A 258

14   St. John The Great Mystic, p. 76

15   Ibid., p. 79

16   Ibid., p. 117

17   The Master Answers, A 253

18   Ibid., A 237

19   Ibid., A 256

20   Ibid., As 420/421

21   Ibid., A 260

22   Kabir The Great Mystic, p. 320

23   Sar Bachan, # 110

24   Ibid., # 189

25   Ibid., # 142

26   Guru Nanak: His Mystic Teachings, p. 315

27   Ibid., p. 387

28   Spiritual Gems, Maharaj Sawan Singh Ji, RSSB. Punjab, India, 1965, L 117

29   Ibid., L 176

30   St. John The Great Mystic, p. 47

31   Ibid., p. 20

32   Spiritual Gems, L 104

33   Sar Bachan. #s 91/92

34   Ibid., # 55

35   Tulsi Sahib, Saint of Hathras, J.R. Puri/V.K. Sethi, RSSB, Punjab, India, 1981, p. 4

Messages from the Masters

36   Ibid., p. 57
37   Ibid., p. 27
38   Guru Nanak, His Mystic Teachings, p. 146
39   Ibid., p. 261
40   Ibid., p. 261
41   Guru Ravidas: Life and Teachings, pp. 65/66
42   Guru Nanak, His Mystic Teachings, p. 231
43   Sar Bachan, # 182
44   St. John, The Great Mystic, p. 39
45   Guru Ravidas: Life and Teachings, p. p. 66
46   Ibid., p. 65
47   Kabir The Great Mystic, p. 249
48   Guru Nanak, His Mystic Teachings, p. 96
49   Ibid., p. 96
50   Ibid., p. 96
51   Ibid., pp. 398/399
52   Ibid., p. 411

Notes

Chapter Four

DIVINE DIET

As we eat, so our mind becomes.
Our food makes our mind.[1]

And God said, Behold I have given
you every herb bearing seed
which is upon the face of all the earth,
and every tree in the which is
the fruit of a tree yielding seed;
to you it shall be for meat.
Bible: Genesis 1:29

Thou shalt not kill.
Bible: The Sixth commandment; *Exodus 20:13*

If we kill, we will be killed.
We should never forget that.[2]
Maharaj Charan Singh Ji

To become vegetarian is to step
into the stream which leads to nirvana.
Buddha

Nothing will benefit human health and
increase chances for survival of
life on earth as much as the
evolution to a vegetarian diet.
Albert Einstein

For a disciple of the *Word of God* there are few things more critical than the food he or she eats. Eating is such a natural act that seldom do we give much thought to it unless we have been blessed with an understanding of compassion for all life. Although eating is a necessary act, <u>what</u> we eat as spiritual seekers, disciples and devotees is, unequivocally, of the most crucial import and acute significance. For one who truly desires to travel the spiritual path he must guard his diet more closely than he guards his wallet or his heart. Money can be replaced; hearts can mend, but the damage done to our spiritual progress by ingesting the wrong foods is frightening and destructive. Contrastingly, by eating the right foods, our spiritual evolution can progress positively. But we must make no mistake--eating can not only be life-preserving, it can also be life-subverting.

Messages from the Masters

The truth of the matter, plainly and clearly, is that one who genuinely desires to return Home to God and Merge in Him *must be a vegetarian.* There is absolutely no other choice. There are no other alternatives. Regarding a vegetarian diet, Perfect Master Maharaj Charan Singh Ji says: *We must follow it. There is no other way for spiritual progress. . . If we kill, we will be killed. We should never forget that. Christ said, "Love thy neighbor". All creatures are our neighbors. . . When you love anybody, you do not kill that individual; and when we love the whole creation, we cannot kill intentionally nor could we find it in our heart to have it done for us by someone else.*[3]

Any message could not be more crystal-clear. When a Perfect Master says of a vegetarian diet, *We must follow it. There is no other way for spiritual progress,* then there is really nothing left to discuss. Saints tell it like it is. They are not concerned about what is politically correct, socially correct, financially correct, psychologically correct, emotionally correct or domestically correct. They are only concerned with what is *spiritually correct.* If one wants to be a true disciple of the *Word of God*; if one wants to return Home to Him, one must follow the dictates of the Master because He *knows* what is spiritually best for the soul's progress and, as we shall also see, Perfect Masters likewise know what the consequences are of not following a vegetarian diet and if those consequences do not scare one to living rightly, then it can be assumed that one's spiritual future will be more one of regress than progress, one of devolution, not evolution.

If we kill, we will be killed. We should never forget that. This is the second part of Saint Charan Singh's message. Why? Because, as we know, the creation is founded upon the precise, exact and inexorable Law of Karma (the law of cause and effect) which mandates that each soul reap what it has sown. *If we kill, we will be killed.* It's as simple as that. And notice the language used. Charan Singh did not say we 'may' be killed or there's a possibility we will be killed. He said, "we *will* be killed." This is as definitive as any statement could ever be.

Yet, who is concerned with this exact fact of life that *if we kill, we will be killed?* As we look around at people and what they eat on a daily basis, especially the exorbitant amount of meat, fish, flesh and fowl they consume multiple times a day, it is incredibly astounding. And just because they eat the meat and perhaps did not directly kill it, does not let them off the hook, to use a gruesome but nonetheless precise pun. Simply purchasing meat at a grocery store is not a legitimate excuse, rationalization or defensible argument which can be raised to invalidate the eating of meat. By buying meat we indirectly contract with someone else to do our killing for us. We are, therefore, complicitous and just as guilty as the butcher. In effect, purchasing meat becomes a contract killing, although it may not be a direct killing. Still, however, the truth remains - we killed, and because we killed, we must be killed in return. We sow; we reap. We sow death, we must reap death. It is *the Law.*

And the third part of Master Charan Singh's statement echoes Christ's statement of "Love thy neighbor." *All creatures are our neighbors.* How could we possibly kill any living thing when we are imbued with love? How could we find it in our hearts to have someone else do it for us?

Maharaj Sawan Singh Ji remarks: *To kill an animal is a heinous offense under natural law and its punishment is very severe. The Saints have strictly forbidden taking any sort of life in any way.*[4] A 'heinous offense'; 'punishment is very severe'! If we're meat eaters, this is not encouraging news, but it is exact news. Hopefully, when one understands the consequences of killing and eating meat, he will, if he is a meat eater, change his life style. Certainly, the penalty will fit the crime, and, to be sure, the benefits *do not* outweigh the risks.

Listen to what another Saint has to say about the killing and eating of meat. Ravidas explains: *By killing the living, O Ravidas, how can God ever be found? Have not Saints, prophets and holy men explained this truth profound? If for the sake of oneself, one goeth to kill another, then reaching the court of the Lord, O*

Ravidas, a severe punishment doth one suffer. Those who eat meat, they, in fact, get their own throats cut. For whosoever is a meat-eater, he will have to go to hell. He who eats meat and fish for the sake of pleasing his palate, he will have his own head severed in return for causing death unnecessarily to a creature.[5]

How sobering is Ravidas' statement! *For whosoever is a meat-eater, he will have to go to hell.* And, *He who eats meat and fish for the sake of pleasing his palate, he will have his own head severed in return for causing death unnecessarily to a creature.*

This is pretty severe punishment. But we must remember that Perfect Saints *know the Truth* because at their extremely advanced spiritual level, they *see the Truth* in operation. Their remarks may frighten us and, hopefully, if we eat meat, frighten us right out of eating it. Saints only come to this earth plane to awaken souls and take them Home. They have no vested interest in the produce business and are not a part of some vegetable and fruit lobby campaign. Their sole purpose is to assist souls in the process of God-realization and this cannot be done when we behave as murderers. Let us not forget the Sixth Commandment of the Holy Bible: *Thou shalt not kill.* And let us also not attempt to put some untoward rationalization, 'spin' or marketing twist on it to justify our own weaknesses, desires and carnal appetites. The directive of the Sixth Commandment is completely clear: *Thou shalt not kill.* And if we do, then Masters simply inform us of the consequences so we may make a more informed choice. And the phrase *thou shalt not kill* does not qualify itself to humans only. *Thou shalt not kill* applies to all living creatures.

Guru Nanak was a staunch believer in vegetarianism. He says: *Countless are the cutthroats who trade in violence; countless are the sinners who thrive on sin and evil; countless are the impious who live on unwholesome food.*[6] Unwholesome food includes, but is not limited to, animal flesh. How complimentary is it to be labeled a cutthroat; to be labeled as one who 'thrives on sin and evil', who 'trades in violence'? Does being a cutthroat make us civilized or uncivilized? Does being a cutthroat make us loving, kind, caring and compassionate or hateful, cruel, uncaring and compassionless?

Maharaj Jagat Singh Ji remarks: *Every day thousands of fowl, sheep, goats, cattle and other animals are killed to provide food for man. Piteous are their agonizing cries, yet, we heed them not. Never have we thought for a moment how we would feel if we were in their place, waiting to be slaughtered. . . How oblivious are we of the pain we cause to animals when we go hunting!*[7]

Jagat Singh hits our heart hard! By engaging in this heinous act of killing and eating meat, he reminds us of how cold, cruel and compassionless we really are. We may think we're loving and caring but to what degree?

If we're true disciples of the *Word of God*, if we truly want to be devoted to the Lord and have Him rescue us from this insidious nightmare of the Wheel of Transmigration, then our love quotient must increase. And that's what Saints are telling us. God's Way is a way of love, not hate; of Life, not death; of joy, not sorrow; of healing, not killing. It is spiritually improper to kill and eat the meat of living creatures. Such activity is inadmissible in the Court of the Lord and frighteningly and tragically perilous to our own well-being.

There is still more powerful deterrent. Saint Ravidas continues: *Those who eat meat, they, in fact, get their own throats cut. For whosoever is a meat-eater, he will have to go to hell, sayeth Ravidas. Having no sense of compassion in their heart, they eat the flesh of another. They are bound to go to hell; truly does Ravidas declare. He who ever eats cows and goats for the sake of nourishing his body, he can never go to heaven, O Ravidas, even if he offers holy prayers day and night. He who eats meat and fish, O Ravidas, for the sake of pleasing his palate, he will have his own head severed in return for causing death unnecessarily to a creature.*[8]

How could anyone with any sense of soulful intelligence, spiritual sentience and heartfelt compassion not be concerned or moved by Ravidas' statement? Obviously, he is poignantly emphatic about those going to hell who eat meat and not going to heaven. And why? Because those who kill God's creatures and eat their flesh are compassionless, and in God's Higher Realms, there is only Love and Life and Light, not cruelty, death and darkness. Even pretending to be holy by offering prayers day and night to God for eating the flesh of His creatures is not compassion enough to stave off the severe penalty of having one's own head severed from his body at some future time in some future life. From a spiritual point of view, one can easily see there is no greater folly than to kill and eat living creatures, and to do so in the name of religion magnifies the foolishness. It is our deeds that count. Not our prayers. In fact, our deeds are our prayers and our consciousness made manifest. If we go about killing and consuming the rotting carcass of animals, where is our Spiritual Light? Our Love? Where is there Life?

Saint Kabir is equally tough on eating meat. He says: *Kill, kill, kill and eat, eat, eat--is the order of the day, and the most astounding part of it is that we have to pay for it. What we kill today will kill us tomorrow.*[9] Again God speaks through another of his Sons and once again the message is the same. The Law of Karma, of Sowing and Reaping, of Cause and Effect, of Compensation and Adjustment comes hurling at us with all the fury of a boomerang in flight: *What we kill today will kill us tomorrow.* When will man get this message? How long will it take him to surrender the ignorance of his blindness and destroy the self-indulgent rationale of his carnal appetites and passions?

Kabir gets even more direct and downright frank. Fearlessly to the point, he takes no prisoners: *O meat-eater,* he says, *you are a devil, not a human being. Keep not a meat-eater's company, for even his company is harmful to devotion for the Lord. Believe me, friend, those who eat meat and fish and drink intoxicating drinks will all be rooted out, like weeds are taken from a fertile field and thrown down into the darksome valley of death. All flesh is one, whether it be of fowl or deer or cow, and those who eat it will go straight to hell with open eyes. You'd not be saved from all the sorrows of hell should you eat even a tiny piece of fish. And I entreat you, take this fact to heart: that he whom you so lightly kill today, will someday slaughter you.*[10]

O meat-eater, you are a devil, not a human being! Talk about tough love! As we can see, Saints pull no punches and they are the toughest of lovers. Their mission is to break us from the bonds of our attachment to this world and destroy the nefarious illusions that keep us deluded and chained to the unholy walls of this dungeon of darkness that we call the world. The Negative Power is the engine behind the killing machine and its propaganda. His purpose is to suppress spiritual Truth. What better way to do this than to make people think there is nothing wrong with eating the flesh of slain animals and that such behavior is normal and natural? Killing is not spiritually natural. It is also not spiritually normal. It is abnormal, a complete aberration.

Kabir also warns us that the quantity of meat consumption is not an issue. The eating of any quantity of flesh bears extreme consequences: *You'd not be saved from all the sorrows of hell should you eat even a tiny piece of fish.* Killing is killing; eating flesh is eating flesh; as you sow so shall you also reap!

Another Perfect Master, Tulsi Sahib (the Saint of Hathras) expounds the same message. He says: *All Saints have extolled the qualities of kindness and mercy. Even the infliction of a minute injury on any living being has been described by them as an act of cruelty. . . All Masters have decried killing and meat-eating. . . Read the Adi Granth carefully; the Gurus have not approved of killing and eating meat anywhere. . . Nanak Sahib was kind and compassionate. He did not permit the killing of animals.*[11]

He strengthens his statement by declaring: *They verily fall into the dungeon of hell who slaughter living beings and eat their flesh. . . For the sake of sensual gratification they buy sin and get their abode in the fires of hell. Whoever has eaten flesh and fish in this life is bound in captivity by the butcher, Kal* [the Negative Power]. *Nothing good will come out of such conduct. Take this as evidence from the writings of Saints. Nanak and Kabir have given the same message; Dadu and Dariya have sung the same song. Tulsi declares from the housetops: kill not the living; within all resides the beloved Lord--listen, O men and women![12]*

Again, another emphatic message! The Bible, too, in its own way echoes the dangers of killing. In the very first chapter of Genesis, verse twenty-nine and *after* God had said that He gave man dominion over all creatures of the earth [verse 28] He said: *Behold, I have given you every herb bearing seed which is upon the face of all the earth, and every tree in which is the fruit of a tree yielding seed; to you it shall be for meat.* In other words it is vegetation upon which you must live, not animals.

As a note, *dominion* does not equate to the right to slay others. Dominion equates to governance, not slaughter. Having *dominion over all the creatures of the earth* simply means man is responsible for caring for all the creatures of the earth and their welfare, not slaughtering them. To slaughter others is an egregious abuse of power and when the karmic backlash occurs, as it definitely will, one will see how little power he has, for his power will be stripped from him in disgrace for his abuse and misuse of it.

Christ said in St. Matthew 5:21--*Ye have heard that it was said by them of old time, thou shalt not kill; and whosoever shall kill shall be in danger of the judgment.* Jesus knew full well that killing was, itself, sowing the seeds of killing and one who killed could not, by karmic law, escape the judgment of certain death. Christ was an extreme advocate of Karmic Law. How often has he

Messages from the Masters

been quoted as saying: *As you sow, so shall you reap*? Yet, why is not this message believed or understood? What more can these Saints and Masters do to convince all of us of the dangers and lethal consequences of killing animals and eating their rotten, decaying, putrescent carcasses?

This raises the question of Christ's own dietary regime. Many people in Christendom believe Christ ate meat. Many people believe he did not. But the salient question is: How could Christ not have been a vegetarian?

When we look at his teachings, we see how he felt about killing and hate and war and evil. He was against all of it. Christ promoted, taught and died preaching a platform of love and compassion. How then could someone so loving, so compassionate, so spiritually enlightened, a pronounced Son of God, be involved in the aimless slaughter, destruction and consumption of animals?

There are hundreds of millions of people in the world who do not eat flesh and the numbers are growing every day. They may not understand the consequences of such heinous acts as outlined by the Perfect Masters quoted above, but many, out of love and compassion for other living creatures, abstain from eating animal flesh. Many do understand and are quite well aware of the karmic consequences of killing and eating other creatures. Suffice it to say these millions of souls do not express the level of Divine Wisdom and Divine Light that Christ Jesus did, so how could such a Master who had been elevated to such a high station in life involve himself with something as low, base, dark and demonic as the killing and eating of animal flesh? It does not make any logical or spiritual sense whatsoever. Therefore, the question of whether Christ was or was not a vegetarian does not arise. The germane question is, "How could Jesus the Christ not have been a vegetarian?"

Actual flesh is not the only issue of importance here. The eating of eggs and the consumption of alcohol and other intoxicating substances is antithetical for one who desires to be a true disciple of the *Word of God.* Maharaj Jagat Singh Ji comments: *Apart from the question of taking life, eggs, whether fertile or infertile are an exciting food, and for persons who engage in spiritual work, non-exciting food is necessary.*[13] Here, Guru Ji is referring to the fact that it is easier to still the mind through the practice of meditation by avoiding the stimulating effect of eggs. Furthermore, eggs are generated in the lower chakras which are not beneficial for one's spiritual development which focuses only on the highest chakras in the human body. He adds: *Meats, eggs and alcoholic drinks scatter the attention and hinder concentration,*[14] and it is concentration which is indispensably vital to focusing the attention in the meditating process.

Messages from the Masters

Maharaj Sawan Singh Ji says: *Meats, eggs and alcoholic drinks have to be given up by the practitioner. They make the spirit coarse and dull.*[15] He offers more advise: *Meats, eggs, and alcohol are poisons and he who uses them will suffer. There is no escape from it.*[16] Of liquor itself he remarks: *The use of liquor is bad. It unsettles the mind and an unsettled mind brings in its train all the evils which one in a normal state avoids.*[17]

Consuming alcohol weakens a person's will to resist sin and travel the higher path. Kabir enjoins: *If you wish to meet the Lord, you must give up all liquor. . . That is the pre-condition. The soul that takes intoxicating drinks will never be taken across to the shore of true salvation. Kabir proclaims with a loud voice and beat of a drum. Consider this statement carefully: abandon all intoxicants.*[18]

This is not rocket-science. It is not social science. It is spiritual science. And it is all a matter of *choice*. Saints are extremely liberal. They never force their ways on anyone. But they do speak pure, unadulterated, spiritual truth. Spiritual success is not about being a good person or a bad person. It's about what *works* spiritually. It is simply a matter of spiritual fact that God doesn't allow a soul into His Higher Kingdoms and Regions of Light unless they have purified themselves to be One with the Spirit. . . His Spirit. Kabir, as well as all Saints, know what is acceptable to the Lord and what is not; what is admissible to the Inner Regions and what is not. This is why Kabir clearly proclaims, *If you wish to meet the Lord, you must give up all liquor. . . That is the pre-condition. The soul that takes intoxicating drinks will never be taken across to the shore of true salvation.*

In the book, Guru Ravidas, Life and Teachings, we read: *One cannot derive proper benefit from the company of Saints and holy men unless one observes the preparatory discipline of self-purification of abstaining from animal food and intoxicating drugs or drinks.* Ravidas makes it quite clear that it is impossible to attain God if one is involved in killing or eating His creatures. *Meat-eaters incur a heavy karmic debt and make God-realization unattainable. Likewise, wine and other intoxicants are also prohibited by Saints.*[19]

Notice in the preceding paragraph the phrase: *preparatory discipline of self-purification.* If we're to ever attain to the level of God-realization, we must be pure; this purity we will achieve by being disciplined. Discipline is the crux of success, and if we're to be spiritually successful, we must develop and maintain a strong and indomitable sense of discipline.

In fact, Saint Jagat Singh remarks: *The Masters say that one should give up all animal food and alcoholic drinks before one is fit to tread the Path.*[20] The emphasis here is on the word, *before.* Hence, if we are truly devoted seekers of God, we must begin to purify ourselves *before* He officially accepts us for Initiation onto the Spiritual Path. In actuality, a Perfect Master will require of his future disciples that they do lead a meat-free, alcohol-free, drug-free life style for some time prior to even applying for Initiation. This is to make certain that seekers are sincere in their desires of dedicating their life to God. Additionally, this pre-initiation trial period is designed to allow seekers the opportunity of ascertaining if, in fact, they can handle the necessary devotional discipline and regimen. After all, once Initiated onto the Spiritual Path by a Perfect Living Master, such a commitment is made for life. There is no turning back.

Reasons for a Vegetarian Diet

Why are Saints adamant advocates of a vegetarian diet? The reason is based on the Law of Karma. The Lord has decreed that killing - the elimination of life from anything[21] - is unacceptable behavior. But this entire world is a killing field with bigger creatures eating smaller, less indefensible ones. Even when we walk and breathe we are killing tiny organisms with every step and breath. It is impossible to live in this creation without killing.

Speaking in this regard, Maharaj Sawan Singh Ji comments: *In our world, life is everywhere destroying life. In such a world where one creature is destroying another, it is impossible to expect either justice or peace of mind. There is no rest or security anywhere. Therefore, when the ancient sages found that in this world creatures were destroying each other, they decided that it was better to give up the world. They found that in such a world there could be no peace of mind; and it was impossible to find peace of mind in any worldly object and that happiness lies within oneself and in that Ocean of which one is a drop. Therefore, the sages thought so long as they were confined in the prison of this world, they would adopt the course which was the least harmful; that is, they would subsist on creatures, the killing of which was the least sinful.*[22]

Every living thing has life in it. Even *every grain, every plant, has life in it.*[23] Says Charan Singh: *Plants have souls, insects have souls, birds have souls, the animals have souls and, of course, human beings have souls.*[24] *The very air you breathe is filled with souls. So it is impossible to live in this world without killing anything. . . We should not try to find a justification for killing, nor should we kill unnecessarily. Where we have to, we may, for we have to in order to live and exist in this world. . . The main thing is that we must do the least killing for our existence - only as much as is absolutely necessary to maintain a healthy body.*[25]

Enter the vegetarian diet. Because every living thing has life in it, every time we kill anything we sin, and because of karmic law we must pay for that sin. Jagat Singh explains: *The karmic load that one has to carry because of killing is in direct proportion to the active elements present in a living being. The larger the number of elements a living entity has, the higher it is in the scale of evolution and, naturally, the greater the onus in killing it. Therefore, Saints enjoin a completely vegetarian diet on their followers. Besides, food of animal origin drags one down to the animal plane and bars spiritual progress.*[26] Thus, not only does eating animal flesh weigh us down, making our spiritual ascent impossible, it also bars us, excludes us, from progressing spiritually.

Saints tell us there are five classifications of living creatures. Each classification is composed of one or more of what Masters call *elements*. These are not to be confused with those chemical elements found in the atomic chart of modern science. The elements to which Masters allude are substances comprising the composition of this cosmic creation. These five ethereal elements are: *water, air, fire, earth and ether.*

Each classification of living creature is comprised of these elements. As Saint Jagat Singh says: *The larger the number of elements a living entity has, the higher it is in the scale of evolution and, naturally, the greater the onus in killing it*, i.e., the greater the karma incurred. Because *the karmic load that one has to carry because of killing is in direct proportion to the active elements present in a living being,* it makes sense that one should kill those creatures that possess the fewest active elements, thereby accruing and incurring the least amount of karmic debt.

As Maharaj Charan Singh Ji remarks: *You can't live in this world without killing. We should try to collect the least amount of karmic load during our life span. If you have a hundred pounds on your head, you are crushed under its weight. But if you have a light frock on, you hardly feel its weight. Collect the least possible load. This comes from vegetables.*[27]

Now let's take a look at the five classifications of living creatures as well as the number and type of elements involved.

Life Classification	Number of Elements	Type of Element
Man	5	earth, water, air, fire and ether
Animals	4	earth, water, air and fire
Birds	3	water, air and fire
Insects	2	air and fire
Vegetables	1	water

As we can see, vegetables only have one element, water. Therefore, by consuming them we incur the least amount of karmic debt possible as we live in this killing field of the world. Since we cannot return Home to God until our entire karmic account is paid off, by eating vegetables, fruits, nuts, legumes, soy and so forth, we keep from accruing more weight-bearing karma. Just as we cannot climb up a mountain with tons of weight strapped to our back, so we cannot also make a spiritual

Messages from the Masters

ascent with tons of karmic debt on our back. And if we keep adding more debt by eating those life forms which naturally incur greater debt, our spiritual success is thwarted and, in fact, impossible. Thus, this is the spiritually scientific reason for being a vegetarian and abstaining from the killing and eating of animals. We simply cannot evolve to higher states of consciousness by following any other dietary regimen. Hence, a vegetarian diet is the *only true* Divine Diet.

A few notes on the vegetarian diet are worthy of mention here. There are basically three types of vegetarians: 1) *Vegan* 2) *Lacto* 3) *Ovo-Lacto*. *Vegans* are pure vegetarians. They eat no animal products whatsoever. *Lacto-vegetarians* may consume dairy products such as cheese and milk as these are products of animals and animals are not slaughtered to acquire them. *Ovo-Lacto* vegetarians eat eggs and dairy. The dietary regimen recommended by Masters is a *Lacto-vegetarian* diet. *Vegan* is, of course, acceptable but *Ovo-Lacto* is not for reasons cited earlier.

Maharaj Sawan Singh makes two additional notes relating to eating and animals. Regarding wearing of animal skins he says: *There is no harm in wearing fur or leather garments, only the killing and eating of living creatures is prohibited.*[28] This goes to the practicality of living in this dimension, notwithstanding the fact that animals do die natural deaths and there is no harm in putting their skins to practical use.

Secondly, regarding fasting, he remarks: *Fasting is not a necessary element to meeting the Lord. It plays no part in the training of the mind and should not be practiced. There is nothing like normality.*[29] What good is achieved by fasting if all we think about is food during our fast? There is certainly nothing wrong with cleansing the body from time to time by fasting, but the real spiritual issue is *training and controlling the mind, concentrating the Attention so the soul can go In.* Fasting has nothing to do with this process. Besides, one can make an excellent argument that abstention from all animal products--meat, fish or fowl, including beef broth, chicken broth, etc. - egg products, alcohol and other intoxicants is a fast in itself.

Summary

The only acceptable dietary regimen for disciples of the *Word of God* is a vegetarian diet. Being a vegetarian means never eating anything that ever had a heartbeat, a face or a mother. This includes broths and sauces made from animals as well as eggs (egg yolks and egg whites). This *Disciple's Diet* also mandates being a teetotaler - one who abstains from all alcoholic drinks and intoxicating substances such as recreational drugs included but not limited to marijuana, cocaine, heroin, crack, speed and so forth.

The *Disciple's Diet* is one suited for the spiritual journey of meeting God face to face. In order to achieve this goal one must be pure in body as well as pure in mind and conduct. There can be no wavering on this dietary issue. It is absolutely obligatory. If one wants to follow a Living Saint and become his disciple in exchange for being liberated from the clutches of this negative environment which is ruled by the Negative Power, the Satan, the Prince of Darkness, the Kal, then one must give up the darkness and negativity of killing and eating the flesh of God's creatures. This is not a request. This is a command.

And why should we not accommodate this vegetarian diet and its subsequent spiritual benefits? As Saint Ravidas queries: *By killing living creatures how can God ever be found? Have not Saints, prophets and holy men explained this truth profound?*[30] He admonishes: *Kill not thou any living beings. Living beings veritably are one with God. . . The sin of killing cannot be washed off.*[31]

And then we must not overlook the consequences of eating animal flesh, consequences given to us quite bluntly by Saints so that there may be no mistaking the message of killing. Remember Tulsi Sahib's declaration: *They verily fall into the dungeon of hell who slaughter living beings and eat their flesh. . . For the sake of sensual gratification they buy sin and get their abode in the fires of hell. Whoever has eaten flesh and fish in this life is bound in captivity by the butcher, Kal* [Satan]. *Nothing good will come out of such conduct. Take this as evidence from the writings of Saints. Nanak and Kabir have given the same message; Dadu and Dariya have sung the same song. Tulsi declares from the housetops: kill not the living; within all resides the beloved Lord. Listen, O men and women!*

Now the reality is that most of us, especially in Western cultures, have eaten meat in this life time. Are we, therefore, bound to Satan as Tulsi Sahib declares? Yes, frankly, unless we quit the heinous crime of killing and eating animal flesh and begin repenting for our misdeeds. As Christ admonished the prostitute in St. John 8:11--*Go and sin no more.* It is by our actions that we will be known and judged, not by our empty words or blind beliefs. The road to hell is paved with good intentions. The road to heaven and beyond is paved with pure conduct and unwavering devotion to God. When God sees that our conduct is in keeping with laws of love and compassion for all life, He graces us with the same and is more forgiving of our past actions. After all, if we're to return Home there comes a definitive time in some life, in some incarnation, when we have to make a shift to live in the light, not the night. God sees all and grants us blessings equal to our behaviors. He knows when we make positive changes from the heart and He rewards those changes with His Grace.

Still, we must be wary and wise in this wicked world. Says Jagat Singh: *To confound people and to entangle them in the karmic complications, nothing beats meat eating and the use of intoxicants.*[32]   As Ravidas remarks: *Saints who have witnessed the Truth declare that one who eats meat will go to hell.   Utterly lowly and devoid of kindness, such a person collects the stinking mud of sins.   Carrying dead bodies of living creatures in his stomach, he is veritably a living corpse.   Furthermore, he adds: There is no greater folly than to kill and eat living creatures in the name of religion.   A meat-eater can never go to heaven even if he offers holy prayers day and night and performs meritorious actions of the highest type.   He will, in fact, come back to this world to settle his account with those creatures whose flesh he has consumed; that is, he will be killed by them.*[33]

So what do we do?   We give up the eating of all animal flesh. . . now, today, not tomorrow.   Every time we eat animals, we *will have to pay the price for our sin* and that piece of chicken, fish, steak, pork or hamburger is just not worth it.   Is it?   *Is it?*   These Saints have given us the truth and as harsh as it may seem, it is a blessing for which to be thankful for it could save us from, as Tulsi Sahib says, the *fires of hell.*

And how do we deal with following a vegetarian diet in a world where meat eating is the course of the day?   Says Maharaj Charan Singh Ji: *I tell you, it is much better to be strong within yourself.   There is no need to feel inferior in this society that we are vegetarian and do not drink, also that we do not serve such things. If people do not really love you, you have no concern with them. Do not bother about them. If they are interested in you, they will respect your principles. They will respect your feelings. And if you think they are not interested in you to that extent, I do not think they are even worth meeting.*[34] *You do not bother about what they* [others] *do. You are to be strict with yourself. You are responsible for yourself. You are not responsible for the world. You cannot solve the problems of the world, but you can rise above those problems and not let them affect you.*[35] *If we kill,* warns Maharaj Charan Singh, *we will be killed. We should never forget that.*

Vegetarian Quotes

It is not only Masters who promote a vegetarian diet. Following are a few quotations from many notable individuals who believe that the eating of meat is inappropriate to a basic sense of human morality.

Pythagoras   *Alas, what wickedness to swallow flesh into our own flesh, to fatten our greedy bodies by cramming in other bodies, to have one living creature fed by the death of another! As long as man continues to be the ruthless destroyer of lower living beings, he will never know health or peace. For as long as men massacre animals, they will kill each other.*

Messages from the Masters

Buddha	*To become vegetarian is to step into the stream which leads to nirvana.*
Albert Einstein	*It is my view that the vegetarian manner of living by its purely physical effect on the human temperament would most beneficially influence the lot of mankind.*
	Nothing will benefit human health and increase the chances for survival of life on earth as much as the evolution to a vegetarian diet.
	Vegetarian food leaves a deep impression on our nature. If the whole world adopts vegetarianism, it can change the destiny of humankind.
Voltaire	*Men fed upon carnage, and drinking strong drinks, have all an impoisoned and acrid blood which drives them mad in a hundred different ways.*
Henry David Thoreau	*I have no doubt that it is a part of the destiny of the human race, in its gradual improvement, to leave off eating animals.*
Robert Louis Stevenson	*We consume the carcasses of creatures of like appetites, passions and organs with our own, and fill the slaughter houses daily with screams of pain and fear. Nothing more strongly arouses our*

disgust than cannibalism, yet we make the same impression on Buddhists and vegetarians, for we feed on babies, though not our own.

George Bernard Shaw

Animals are my friends...and I don't eat my friends.

We are the living graves of murdered beasts slaughtered to satisfy our appetites.

Mohandas Gandhi

I do not regard flesh-food as necessary for us at any stage and under any clime in which it is possible for human beings ordinarily to live. I hold flesh-food to be unsuited to our species. We err in copying the lower animal world - if we are superior to it.

To my mind, the life of a lamb is no less precious than that of a human being. I should be unwilling to take the life of a lamb for the sake of the human body.

Paul McCartney

If slaughterhouses had glass walls, everyone would be vegetarian. We feel better about ourselves and better about the animals, knowing we're not contributing to their pain.

Thomas Edison

Until we stop harming all other living beings, we are still savages." ... "I am vegetarian and I don't

Messages from the Masters

drink in order to make better use of my brain.

Leo Tolstoy   *Flesh eating is simply immoral, as it involves the performance of an act, which is contrary to moral feeling: killing.*

If a man earnestly seeks a righteous life, his first act of abstinence is from animal food.

Leonardo da Vinci   *If man wants freedom why keep birds and animals in cages? Truly man is the king of beasts, for his brutality exceeds them. We live by the death of others. We are burial places! I have from an early age abjured the use of meat, and the time will come when men such as I look upon the murder of animals as they now look upon the murder of men.*

One Final Note

It's impossible to speak of love, let alone be loving, follow the spiritual path and consume flesh. In all ways such behavior is contradictory. Love promotes life. Eating flesh promotes death . . . and cannibalism. The spiritual path of love is saturated in Spirit. Meat eating is saturated in matter. There is no matter in Spirit. We simply cannot ascend the ladder of life by eating flesh. How can we legitimately seek life when we immerse our consciousness and fill our bodies with death? Life begets life; love begets love; death begets death. It is the law.

Animal Food

© Richard Andrew King

Animal food to animal plane;

omnivorous, carnivorous diet: dangerous game.

We cannot Ascend to Spiritual Planes,

when slaughtering animals for selfish gains.

The Way of the Spirit is Spirit True.

Consuming flesh will consume you.

Negative karma do we accrue,

when we the carcass of animals chew.

Forever will we be forlorn

when we our heads with flesh adorn.

Forever will we have to morn,

for eating those of mother born.

Personal choice is fine to make

but it would be a grave mistake,

to think our thoughts the Law forsakes,

when we the lives of creatures take.

No one escapes the act of killing.

No one thought perhaps more chilling,

than paying recompense for the filling

of our bowels with the blood we're spilling.

Messages from the Masters

Critical to Freedom, this feeding game;
'tis but ourselves we have to blame
when we cannot our diets tame.
Our lot - to suffer just the same.

Consider why the world suffers.
Slaughtering children of their mothers
and eating their flesh most surely colors
the karmas we reap from eating others.

Think you'll escape? Think again.
Consuming flesh is *tragic* sin.
Horrific penalties accrue to him
or her who is not vegetarian.

Eating Meat

© Richard Andrew King

It is dietary suicide
this act of eating meat--
the killing of the spirit,
replete with all the tending evils
a murderer will meet
when he receives his judgment
at the Great Assessor's feet.

The Law's exact, inexorable--
we harvest what we plant,
and when we plant these killing seeds,
then killing is our grant.

There's no great secret here:
when we kill to feed our lust,
the principles which form the Law
return to feed on us.

When we plant death and killing,
it's death and killing that we get--
perfect compensation for the
fruits our seeds beget.

As the father sires the son,
and the flames the fingers burn,
so the sentence for our murdering
is to be murdered in return.

Laugh and smile while we may,
but the Books will all be balanced.
The penalty for eating meat
is that our life is silenced.

Think not belief will save our soul,
the Law cannot be stilled.
The consequence for eating meat
is that *we* will be killed.

And we *will* suffer, and we *will* cry;
in ignorance we *will* weep
until we learn to *live* the Law
that what we sow, we reap!

Bibliography: Chapter Four

1   *The Science of the Soul*, Maharaj Jagat Singh Ji, Radha Swami Satsang Beas, P. 200
2   *The Master Answers*, Maharaj Charan Singh Ji, Radha Swami Satsang Beas, p. 293
3   Ibid., p. 293
4   *Spiritual Gems*, Maharaj Sawan Singh Ji, RSSB, L 154
5   *Guru Ravidas: Life and Teachings*, K.N. Upadhyaya, RSSB, 1982, pp. 67/68
6   *Guru Nanak, His Mystic Teachings*, Professor J.R. Puri; RSSB, 2 edition, 1982, p. 102
7   *The Science of the Soul*, p. 57
8   *Guru Ravidas*, pp. 194/195
9   *Kabir The Great Mystic*, Professor J.R. Puri, RSSB, 2nd edition, 1982 p.101
10   Ibid., pp. 412/413
11   *Tulsi Sahib, Saint of Hathras*, J.R. Puri/V.K Sethi, RSSB, 1981, p. 17
12   Ibid., pp. 67-69
13   *The Science of the Soul*, p. 165
14   Ibid., p. 200
15   *Spiritual Gems,* LL 148/150
16   Ibid., L 80
17   Ibid., L 80
18   *Kabir The Great Mystic*, p. 411
19   *Guru Ravidas: Life and Teachings*, pp. 67/68
20   *The Science of the Soul*, p. 165
21   *Speech by Maharaj Charan Singh Ji,* 22 June 1975, Bloomsbury Centre Hotel, London, England, videotape
22   *Spiritual Gems*, L 179
23   Ibid., L 154
24   *The Master Answers*, A 387
25   Ibid., A 579
26   *The Science of the Soul*, p. 71
27   *22 June 1975 Speech, Maharaj Charan Singh Ji*
28   *Spiritual Gems*, L 192
29   Ibid., L 42
30   *Guru Ravidas: Life and Teachings*, p. 192
31   Ibid., p. 193
32   *The Science of the Soul*, p. 126
33   *Guru Ravidas: Life and Teachings*, p. 194
34   *The Master Answers*, A 296
35   Ibid., A 298

Chapter Five

THE HUMAN FORM

Know ye not that ye are the temple of God,
and that the spirit of God dwelleth in you?[1]

How strange is it that mankind moves from cradle to grave in his divinely gifted human form seldom, if ever, questioning the purpose of his body? It is a question defying explanation. Man asks this human body to do many things for him: pleasure him, sustain him, create for him, procreate for him, recreate for him, entertain him, destroy for him, kill for him and even digest the slain rotting, decaying carcass of other beasts for him which lay decomposing within the very depths of his ostensibly insatiable bowels, creating a stench which is not only glaringly repugnant but which is also quite unworthy of the divine man that dwells within him. Never, however, does it seem that man gives his body, his human form, more thought beyond that which his carnal instincts require.

Always, it seems, he uses it for the sole purpose of gratifying, supporting, expressing and manifesting everything that is purely animal and blatantly base, often excusing or rationalizing such behavior as a biological function only.

How strange, indeed! Man, at least in some quantities and degrees, seems to recognize the reality of God. He goes to church; to temple; to mosque. He prays. He seeks to do good works. He reads. He educates himself regarding worldly interests. He's been taught well in many fields of endeavor. He's accomplished many worldly things, expanded his technology, even propelled his human kind into outer space.

Yet, for all his worldly activity and accomplishment, he ignores, or chooses not to act upon, the one piece of spiritual fact that has been taught by every Mystic Saint since the beginning of time and that can forever liberate him from the illusion and darkness of his captivity within the fearsome and foreboding walls of the labyrinthine nightmare that is this world - and that spiritual fact is that his body, his human form, is not only the *Temple of God*, the *Living God*, but that God himself dwells within it and it is within this form, and only in this form, that the soul has the supreme and supernal opportunity of realizing God through it.

However, quite sadly, by refusing to honor and act upon this divine fact, man has desecrated his body temple and made it into a repository of death rather than a temple of Living Love, Life and Light. With all of his accomplishments, man, certainly cannot be called stupid, so how is it that he should overlook the most potent and grand reality of his human body, his human form? Is it, in fact, ignorance that victimizes man so? Is it arrogance? Is it simply careless oversight? Myopic indifference? Perhaps even indigent lethargy? Or, is it spiritual blindness, blindness caused by a mind so enshrouded by illusion and darkness that it simply cannot see nor perceive the great and rare reality that dwells, not right in front of his very face, but even closer, closer than his own breath? Indeed, that rare reality lies inside the very body which he carries around with him every day. It waits there, and has been waiting ever so patiently for man to wake up from his sorry state and reclaim the spiritual dignity he lost and keeps losing by stumbling and fumbling around in the banal and baneful morass of this cesspool of a place that is called the world, a world where all life lives on death and destruction.

A Perfect Saint in the form of Maharaj Jagat Singh Ji, who taught the secrets of spiritual mysticism up until his transition in 1951, asks simply: *Have we ever given thought to our body? How wonderful is the twelve-storied house in which we live?*[2] By twelve stories he was referencing the twelve primary chakras which operate within the human frame--energy vortices comprising the spiritual-cosmic composition of man.

Viewing these from the bottom upwards, the first six chakras begin from the rectum (the lowest chakra) and proceed to the reproductive center [2], then to the solar plexus [3], heart [4], throat [5] and Eye Center [6] which is located just above the two physical eyes and behind the centerpoint between the eyebrows.[3]   This sixth chakra is the *Third Eye* referenced in mystic and metaphysical literature. It is the Doorway to the Inner Spiritual Realms, the Tenth Gate and the true starting point of the spiritual journey *Within*. The second six chakras exist within the cranial area and represent energy vortices of higher internal spiritual regions.

Spiritually speaking, says Jagat Singh, *the human body may be divided into two parts. One part is from the soles of the feet to the eyes, and the other is from the eyes up to the top of the head. The lower part, including the eyes, is meant to function in this material world. This is known to common man. But what is not known to most people is that the upper part is meant to connect the soul and the mind with higher regions.*[4]

He continues: *The human body is a laboratory for spiritual research and proof can be had by taking the attention inside... There is intense light within you as are also numberless planes where unceasing music is going on. . . When the attention has gone in, one meets with prophets and sages at different planes, even though they died long, long ago.*[5]

How could Jagat Singh know this? Because he was a Perfect Saint, a Son of God who came into the world, as do all Sons of God, to rescue souls from this world and take them Home to God Himself. Guru Nanak, who lived in the Fifteenth Century and was born in 1469 AD, was one of the most famous Perfect Saints of India. He says: *Precious is this human birth; only the Saints know its worth.*[6] *Not only does God live within the human body, but it is only within this body that He [God] manifests Himself. Thus it is doubly blessed.*[7]

Guru Nanak and Maharaj Jagat Singh are saying nothing new. All Saints are One and spring from the same Divine Source. Their message is the very message that Christ Jesus taught who, through a query to his disciples, remarked: *Know ye not that ye are the Temple of God, and that the Spirit of God dwelleth in you?*[8]

Why do Saints place such priceless value on the human body, the human form? Why are they so insistent that we know that our human frame *is* the Temple of the Living God? And why would Guru Nanak make a point of saying that it is *only within this body that God manifests Himself?* Are there other bodies?

The Wheel of Transmigration

Mystics tell us that, as humans, we live within the confines of a great spiritual-cosmic structure of eight million, four hundred thousand [8,400,000] cells or body forms into which our souls can incarnate; that as souls we have been living in and transmigrating within the boundaries of this vast prison house for eons, millions of years, passing from life form to life form in a limitless number of incarnations; rising and falling, living and dying, coming and going to the ceaseless rhythm of the great cosmic pendulum, all the time being tossed back and forth in a tide of pain and pleasure, joy and sorrow, tragedy and triumph. Names for this structure of 8,400,000 thousand species of forms are *Chaurasi*, the *Wheel of Eighty-Four*, the *Wheel of Transmigration*.

Transmigration is the process by and through which our soul moves through and acquires different kinds of forms and bodies in response to our conduct and consciousness during our existence in this creation. The soul does not die. It is the essence of the Supreme Lord. But the physical covering of our soul can change from life to life, and does according to our actions in each life, according to our *karmas*. Through the process of *reincarnation* - the taking on of a new body from life to life - we are placed at various levels of being in each of our incarnations, in each of our lives. The Wheel of Transmigration is the configuration housing the millions of forms, bodies and structures into which our soul is deposited, incarnated and reincarnated.

Some people may doubt the reality of reincarnation. However, Sawan Singh, a Perfect Saint of the Twentieth Century, says quite directly and irrefutably, *The principle of reincarnation is a fact. It is part of the Creator's scheme.*[9]   Even the Bible, which has been plagued by numerous translations and manipulations throughout history, gives indirect mention to reincarnation, but mention nonetheless. We read in St. Matthew, Chapter 16, verses 13 and 14: *When Jesus came into the coasts of Caesarea Philippi, he asked his disciples, saying, Whom do men say that I am? And they said, Some say that thou art John the Baptist; some, Elias; and others Jeremias, or one of the prophets.*

Now why would Christ's disciples answer such a question in this way? Elias is the Greek form of Elijah, a reference to Elijah the Prophet mentioned in the Old Testament of the Bible and living long before Jesus was born, as did Jeremias and the other prophets mentioned by Christ's disciples. This passage clearly indicates that Christ and his disciples had a working understanding of reincarnation, otherwise their answers would make no sense. Too, we must remember that Christ was an Eastern Mystic and the principle of reincarnation is a known and accepted fact in Mystic teachings.

Even modern science teaches that energy can neither be created nor destroyed. The soul is pure energy. It, therefore, cannot be destroyed. But it can be covered with different types of 'clothing', raiment, i.e. bodies. When we die, we do not really die. Our physical, material body dies but the soul does not. It cannot. It simply exits one body and enters another, moving through the experience of its existence, acquiring the type of form or covering for which it is best suited to play out its karma, its action. If its action and desire field are saturated with animal lusts, instincts and actions, it is given the form of some animal. If its conduct has been heinous and overtly negative, it can even be given a lesser form - that of a bird, fish, insect or plant. Likewise, if its actions have been positive while living in lower life forms and cumulative enough, it is given the form of a man, a human being. Thus, the soul, having passed through many different types of bodies and accumulating enough good karma, is granted the human form. This is no small achievement. In fact, Saints tell us it is quite rare.

Of these 8,400,000 forms, man is the absolute highest form. He occupies the top rung of the ladder of creation. He is the *crème de la crème* of living beings with bodies. But he did not gain this prestigious position easily. Says Maharaj Jagat Singh Ji: *The human form, which is our most precious gift and which we have obtained after wandering through the eighty-four Lac species* [one Lac equals 100,000] *is the top of creation. It is wise to put it to appropriate use and rise above the domain of Kal* [Kal is the negative power, the Devil, Satan].[10]   He reiterates: *Man is the top of creation and if his deeds are those of a man, he will continue to advance. However, if he stoops to lower actions like those of animals, birds or insects, he is bound to become what he made himself while in the form of man.*[11]

We notice from these two previous quotes that the human body is a *gift* from God, a gift to *use* appropriately. It is not a right to have a human body. It is a privilege, a gift, given to us for the purpose of advancing our soul's liberation and salvation. Contrary to popular belief, we do not own our bodies. They belong to God and He loans them to us for the purpose of advancing our soul Homeward. How we use our body on a personal level is, therefore, critical, and if we misuse it we will have to pay the consequences by being sent down into the Wheel, into lower forms of life. Thus, our human life and its opportunity of God-realization, have extreme and critical spiritual significance for each of us. To use the human body solely in the pursuit of worldly activity, pleasure, sensation, gain, gratification and amusement is not only a total waste of time, but perilously dangerous. It thus becomes of paramount importance that we understand the purpose of life in the human form - that of seeking God and realizing Him. To become absorbed in His creation is the sure guarantee of staying *in* the creation. However, if we want to get out of the creation and return to Him and our true Home, we must become more seriously minded in relation to this human body, this human form and what we do with it. We've all heard the saying, "use it or lose it." Well, if we do not use the human body for the great spiritual purpose of merging with our Creator, we *will* lose it (our body) and not only that, but have to suffer the ignominy of being sent down into the Wheel where only darkness and suffering exist. It is the tragedy of all tragedies, surpassing even the reverential pen of the Great Bard, William Shakespeare.

Guru Ji also said this human body is to be used to *rise above the domain of the negative power.* This statement is clearly indicative of where we currently reside. We talk about 'this place' as being ruled by the Prince of Darkness, but do we really realize it? Do we truly understand what darkness is? Do we appreciate that darkness is not merely a reference to a condition absent of light, but that darkness is also a definition of *ignorance*, a lack of knowledge, awareness or comprehension? Do we not comprehend or know there is more to creation than *this* world, *this* life, *this* dimension, *this* human form? From Guru Ji's comment, it is equally indicative that there is someplace of higher quality because he said that the purpose of the human form is given to us so we can rise above this world. Obviously, there is some place of far greater experience than *this* world!

Guru Arjan was a Perfect Saint and also one of the Ten Sikh Gurus whose writings comprise part of the *Granth Sahib* or *Adi Granth* - a famous Indian holy book on par with the Christian Bible. On this issue of reincarnation and transmigration he states: *Many lives hast thou passed as insects and moths; many as elephants, fish and deer; for many lives wert thou bird and serpent, and for many horse and tree. Oh seek God now! This is the time of union with the Lord, for after a long time hast thou got the human form.*[12]

Guru Ji, Maharaj Jagat Singh, further explains: *Family, parents, children we had in every life. Food, sleep, lust and greed are also common to all forms. The unique quality in human life which is not present in other forms, is the capacity for God-realization and permanent release from the prison-house of Chaurasi. The rare privilege is not bestowed upon any other species. This is the time to seek a Master, learn the technique from Him* [regarding spiritual ascent and God-realization] *and reach our Eternal home whence we do not return to this world again.*[13]

Saint Kabir testifies: *[The] human body is hard to obtain. One doth not get it again and again. When a ripe fruit falleth from a tree, never again doth it return to the branch.*[14] Through this passage we receive corroboration of the precariousness, and yet preciousness, of the human body, the Temple of God. Kabir is emphatic on the point that this human body is *hard to obtain* and that we *do not get it again and again.* This Saint's statement also carries with it a sense of urgency and utter import. Because this human body only comes to us very rarely, we must not only not abuse it or misuse it, we must use it in divinely appropriate ways or we will lose it and suffer greatly because of our careless stupidity. After all, how many of us have the ability to reattach and replace a piece of fruit which has fallen from a tree? None of us, and when our fruit, our human body, has fallen from the tree of this life, i.e. when it dies, it will not be reattached unless we take spiritually positive action *now* to insure our future progress.

Huzur Swami Ji Maharaj, the founder of Sant Mat, the Science of the Soul which expounds the teachings of Perfect Saints, explains: *The human body is short-lived. It is not worthwhile feeling proud of its youth and beauty. As trees lose their leaves in the autumn, likewise this youth and beauty also will be gone in a few days. Therefore, we should not waste it away but find a beloved Master and devote our time to service and attendance on Him.*[15]

Most of us blindly think we will live forever. Life seems long, especially if we're young. But wait until we're old. Life will seem short. We will look back on our life and wonder where it all went and how it could have possibly passed away so quickly.

Messages from the Masters

Likewise, many of us think we're indestructible. However, when we're seriously injured, maimed or permanently disabled, or when we see a close loved one or friend die, the reality of our mortality weighs heavy in our gut and our sense, our false sense of indestructibility and immortality, wanes, as well it should. When the youth, beauty and vibrancy we once possessed which brought us energy, fun, excitement, praise, adoration, attention, perhaps even wealth and fame, wastes away leaving us with old age, insipid non-vitality and physical unattractiveness, we often become quite sobered, if not even angry, bitter and resentful. Like the fruit falling from the tree, the leaves of our tree of life will one day wither, die and fall. It is the nature of the cycle of life. Swami Ji is simply reminding us of reality and exhorting us to become aware of it and modify our goals and objectives to deal with it in *this life, now.*

He goes on to say: *Not to seek the True God but to worship His creation as God Himself and to worship the things which man himself has made - how much does it speak for the negligence, ignorance and carelessness of the people? How sinful for one endowed with such a precious body to so degrade himself that he becomes fit only to descend into hell or into lower forms of life instead of making use of that body to ascend to the Lord Himself.*[16]

There is a difference between the Creator and His creation. As Christ Jesus told his disciples in St.

Matthew, Chapter 22, verses 37, 38: *Thou shalt love the Lord thy God with all thy heart, and with all thy soul, and with all thy mind. This is the first and great commandment.* Jesus said, love the Lord God first and foremost. This is the *first* and *great* commandment. In other words, love the Creator *first* and *foremost.* Jesus did not say, 'love the creation first.' He said love God first. But so often we get it backwards. We love the world first, its activity and people. Erroneously we believe that if we love His creation first - His people, things and activities - we are loving Him first. We are not. We have inverted the truth as well as deceived and fooled ourselves. We have made ourselves *negligent, ignorant* and *careless.* In effect, we have, as Swami Ji says, degraded ourselves, and the sad consequence for our misguided focus is that we will be descended into hell or into lower forms of life. And we do so because it is much easier to love the creation than loving the Creator. The former allows us to play, while the latter demands devotion which translates into discipline, restraint, commitment, a rejection of worldly pleasure and sensation, sacrifice, surrender and . . . long suffering. It is not easy to truly love the Lord, our Creator. It is much easier just to talk about it, or rationalize it, or pretend we are doing it but, all the while, acting and conducting ourselves differently and behaving quite badly. Unfortunately for most of us, we fail to realize that God can neither be deceived nor fooled. He knows who is really worshipping Him and who is not and rewards, disciplines or punishes us accordingly.

Swami Ji further comments: *This valuable human body you got after roaming in millions of lower lives. Now do not lose it in vain pursuits. Take heed! Give your attention to Devotion. Have pity on your poor soul and save it from transmigration's wheel. These pleasures and comforts are for four days. After that a long period of sorrow awaits you. Beware! Save yourself from hell-fire; do not make your soul its fuel!*[17]

Whew! *Take heed! Beware! Save yourself from hell-fire; do not make your soul its fuel!* It seems these are echoes of Jonathan Edwards' "Sinners in the Hands of an angry God" sermon. The fact is, such statements are true. Saints *know* about life in all of its aspects. They are so advanced they can see the past, present and future of anyone and anything. They are not con-men. They do not come to deceive nor make of this life a paradise on earth. They come to awaken souls, to educate them as to the reality of *this* world, *this* creation and its structure, to free these souls from the real bondage and darkness in which they live and dwell and by which they have been blinded for eons and return them home to their true Home in the higher regions of the Lord's Inner Sanctum. When Swami Ji or any Saint passionately proclaims, *Take heed! Beware! Save yourself from hell-fire; do not make your soul its fuel!*

he means it. It is the truth, and if we do not accept it or act upon it, then when the time comes and we find ourselves being sucked down into the abysmal depths of hell and forced to live life as something less than a human, we have no one to blame but ourselves and fie on us! Who can have sympathy for someone who hears but remains heedless? This is our life and it is our responsibility. It is time to understand the immense value of the human form and the equal responsibility it conveys. If we do not, then "Oh, well!" What can be said? In such a case, Saint Kabir's words ring loudly and clearly: *What can they know, these worldly fools, these fools, fools, fools?*[18]

The Bible echoes these thoughts as well. In St. Matthew (7:19) we read: *Every tree that bringeth not forth good fruit is hewn down and cast into the fire. Every tree* is a reference to the individual soul, the soul which does not reflect the goodness (Godness) of human life. And what happens to these "trees?" They're cut down, destroyed and thrown into the fire. Ever been burned? It's not a pleasant experience is it? Is this the kind of experience we want to have when our life ends?

We also read in St. Matthew 13: 41-42: *The Son of man shall send forth his angels, and they shall gather out of his kingdom all things that offend, and them which do iniquity and shall cast them into a furnace of fire: there shall be wailing and gnashing of teeth.* "Cast into a furnace of fire!" "There shall be wailing and gnashing of

Messages from the Masters

teeth!" Sound pleasant? Can you imagine such a fate? Do we really think that just because life is good now, it will always be this way? We need to awaken to the messages these masters are sending. If we don't, we cannot blame God when the fire comes . . . and burns. God is telling us through these Mystics and their messages that now, while we occupy the highest rung on the evolutionary ladder; while we have a human form and are capable of understanding the truth; while we have been blessed with such a gift, that we need to get a grip on the essence of what is truly real from a spiritual standpoint, to act on that knowledge, and to act on it *now*, before it is too late. Once the fruit falls from the tree, it cannot be put back. As Kabir says, *Worship the Supreme Lord before doing anything else. Why do you remain unconcerned with this fact? When will you again get such a lucky chance? Remember, you will not get such a body again for ages and then you will repent most bitterly. Incomparable is the human life. In the Wheel of Eighty-four lacs of births whether thou art a king or a beggar, wake up to this one duty. Remain not unconcerned, I warn thee!*[19]

Higher than Gods & Angels

As Saints tell us, man is the top of creation. That means all creation within the physical, astral and causal regions. He even occupies a place and status higher than angels and gods who reside in and rule over these

134

regions. Great Master (Maharaj Sawan Singh Ji) notes: *Man is the highest form of creation including the angels.*[20] *It is given to man [human beings] only to rise upward. In no other form, not even that of angels, is this possible. Man is the top of creation.*[21]

The angels, says Great Master, *are simply living life in Paradise in the Astral Plane and are enjoying the fruits of the good actions that they performed in human life, and when that period is over, they, too, will be reborn as men and their further course will be determined by the sort of actions they will perform then. The point is, the angels have not the capacity to unite with the Creator. This capacity is given to man and man alone and therein lies his greatness.*[22]

How this, once again, drives home the incredible importance and weight the human form carries in the macrocosmic view of the creation. Isn't it true that most people think of angels as occupying a higher place in the divine order of things than mere humans? But no. Such is not the case. *The angels have not the capacity to unite with the Creator. This capacity is given to man and man alone and therein lies his greatness.*

Saint Kabir relates the same information. *Even,* he says, *the gods and goddesses pine for the human body, for within this body resideth the Lord Himself.*[23] The word *pine* means to *yearn intensely and persistently for something unattainable.*[23] If even these beings, whom we normally regard as more evolved than we mere mortals, 'yearn intensely and persistently' for that which they do not have, which to them is unattainable, but something which we do have, how special does that make us as beings in current possession of a human body? That's why Christ emphatically queries his disciples: *Know ye not that your body is the temple of the Holy Ghost which is in you, which ye have of God?*[25] And in case this was not clear to them, in case they somehow overlooked the rhetorical nature of his question, he moves beyond, asking his disciples if they know this truth and he tells them point blank: *Ye are the temple of the Living God.*[26]

Christ knew the value of the human form just as all Saints. This is why all of them are so dynamically emphatic in helping us understand the great unparalleled truth of the human form. We are the temple of the Living God. This temple is the form central to our soul's liberation, eternal salvation, escape and freedom from the dungeon of darkness of the Devil's domain. But what is it exactly that makes the human body, the human form, so different, so special that even gods and goddesses pine for it?

Body of Ten Doors

The human body is special because of all the 8,400,000 bodies that God has created for the placement of his souls, the human body alone possesses a secret passageway allowing the being housed within it to

escape to Freedom and return Home.   This secret
passageway exists in no other form.   Therefore, when a
soul finally receives the rare chance of dwelling within it
for a few years, it has the golden opportunity of escaping
from the Wheel of Transmigration and evolving inward
and upward through the inner regions with the grace of a
Perfect Master to its original Home and place of eternal
rest and true immortality.

But this golden opportunity is very short.   Human
life may seem like a long time, but it is not.   Seventy,
eighty or ninety years of human longevity when
juxtaposed with the eons of time our soul has been
transmigrating within the Wheel is, comparatively, just a
few heartbeats in length.   And no one really knows when
he or she will die.   Many people die young.   But, of
course, they never thought it would happen to them, that
they should die so early, so young.   And the cost: loss of
the chance to escape forever from the Wheel, resulting in
continued bondage, incarceration, slavery, pain and
suffering within it.   Hence, the impassioned exhortations
of Saints to get busy with spiritual work *now* because
spiritual work can only be effective *in the human form.*
Says Saint Jagat Singh: *Take heed! This work can be
accomplished only in the human form. Therefore, take
full advantage of this opportunity for it is the greatest
good fortune to be born as a human being after long and
tortuous wanderings in other lives. You have a short
span of life and this, too, is running out fast. Unless you*

wake up now, it will be futile to cry over split milk later.[27] *Every time*, says Guru Ji, *we [mortals] get the gift of the human form, instead of utilizing it for God-realization, we turn to sensual pleasures and once again go down into the labyrinth* [the Wheel of Transmigration].[27]

This human birth, possessing this human body - this Temple of the Living God - is so critical to our experience and spiritual evolution that Swami Ji Maharaj soberingly declares: *Those who now have a human body but do not seek the Sat Guru* [the Living Master of the time] *will go to Chaurasi and will not get the human form again [this is subject to certain conditions]. It is time, therefore, to gain your release now and if you lose this opportunity, you will not get it again.*[29]   Therefore, *now, now* is *the* time for us to wake up, clean up our consciousness, clean up our acts, behaviors and conducts and get busy with the spiritual work of God-realization. Not tomorrow, not next week, nor next month, nor next year but *now. Now*!

This returns us to the secret passageway that God has given to the human form and it alone. Most highly evolved animals have basically nine outlets in their physical forms through which they function and are also tied to the material creation. These are the two eyes, two ears, two nostril openings, the mouth and the two lower outlets of elimination and procreation. Saints refer to these as the *nine doors*. But the form of man, the form in which we currently but may not always reside, has ten. The *tenth door* is the secret passageway of escape. Through it, with the help of a Perfect Master, the soul can extricate itself from the bondage of this world and the negative power can do nothing about it. Once through this door with the guidance and protection of a Living Saint, the soul is home free, destined to live an eternal life of indescribable joy, peace and bliss within the Kingdom of God.

Where is this passageway, this Tenth Door? It is the Third Eye, that mystical opening which is found above the physical eyes and behind the centerpoint of the eyebrows. It is here that the secret passageway to God's inner realms exist. It is here that man's spiritual salvation begins. And it exists in the human form and no other.

It is also here, through this secret passageway, this Tenth Gate, that the light of the inner worlds is perceived. This is why Christ said: *The light of the body is the eye: therefore, when thine eye is single, thy whole body also is full of light.*[29] Notice that Christ did not use the word "eyes". He said, 'eye.' 'Eye' is singular, not plural. It is this 'Third Eye' which all mystics know is the opening to the spiritual kingdom of God, the secret passageway to the inner realms and the portal of escape from the Wheel of Transmigration.

Now Christ also said, *when thine eye is <u>single</u>.* What he meant by using the word *single* was that when this Third Eye is *concentrated*, when the *attention* is so focused within it, then, and only then, will the body be full of light. It is at this time of singleness that the attention is withdrawn from the outer world via the lower nine outlets and concentrated at the organ of spiritual awareness where the *light journey* begins. This is why Guru Ji says: *The human body is the body of ten gates: nine open outward into the phenomenal world and one opens inward to the Way of the Palace of the Lord within.*[31]

Material, modern, worldly science does not know of this secret door, nor can it. Worldly science is of the mind, and the mind is limited and knows nothing of the spirit within. The Tenth Door is an aperture of the spirit and therefore falls within the realm of soul science. The soul, not the mind, is capable of perceiving the Spirit. Masters are the Ph.D.s of the Spirit and all of its knowledge, which is why we must seek their counsel, their teachings, their guidance, their expertise if we are to make any gains in life which are spiritual in nature.

The Gate Keeper

Knowing of the reality of this Tenth Door, this secret passageway to the inner spiritual worlds, is not enough. In order to open it and *proceed through it safely*, one needs a guide, a protector who has been through the gate and traversed the secret passageway *all the way Home.* To enter this gate alone and unprotected poses a great hazard for the soul and should never be done unless one has the omnipotent protection of a Master Guide. That Master guide is the Living Master, the Perfect Saint. Without him, the journey within, which can be accomplished for a short distance, is fatefully perilous. The inner regions are fraught with extreme dangers for the soul, and an unprotected sojourn there will only end in disaster. For this reason, one must seek the Living Saint of the time and devote himself or herself to his teachings and to him. To do so spells success and ultimate triumph. Not to do so will only spell failure and immense tragedy for the soul.

This is why Christ said: *No man cometh unto the Father but by me.*[32] He did not mean 'me' the personality Jesus. He meant 'me' the living Master of my time. This is confirmed by Maharaj Jagat Singh Ji who states: *It is impossible to undertake the journey inside without a Perfect Guide.*[33] He also says: *It is only with the grace of a living Satguru* [Perfect Saint] *that we can close the nine doors, still the mind, enter the Tenth one and contact Nam* [the Word of God mentioned in St. John which is the voice of God] *which constantly resounds there. This is the only way. None else exists.*[34]

Summary

The human body is the Temple of the Living God. It is the vehicle for our spiritual salvation. But it, the

Messages from the Masters

human body and our existence within it, are short lived. Improper use of it and improper use of our time spent in it will yield only tragic and devastatingly negative effects for us. *Therefore,* says Swami Ji, *we should not waste it away but find a beloved Master and devote our time to service and attendance on Him. There is no loss if one's entire life is spent in seeking a Sat Guru* [a Perfect Living Master]. *On the other hand, it is very beneficial because it entitles the seeker to human life the next time. If, however, he takes to pilgrimages, fasts, image worship, display of supernatural powers, mental magic and ritualistic worship. . . and the like, the right to human birth also is forfeited and the individual is thrown back into the cycle of transmigration. Those who are eager to escape transmigration should believe in the teachings of the Saints and make proper use of this human life which has been obtained after much difficulty. It should not be wasted. But if one will not believe, he is free to follow his own course.*[35] Soberingly, Swami Ji poignantly declares: *If you don't believe in either what I say or in the writings of the Saints, the path of Transmigration lies before you. Walk upon it by all means.*[36]

Human Life

© Richard Andrew King

This human life is priceless--
its value set by Him,
a value more expensive
than a host of Seraphim;
a treasure more exquisite
than a cavalcade of gods
strolling through some golden gate
on a starlit promenade.
This body is the only form
wherein the Lord resides,
a form adorned with Godliness
in the realm above the eyes.
It is the only vehicle
where man can make escape
from the Devil and his minions
whose job it is to rape
the soul and keep it
trapped within his den
where all are blind and helpless
and ignorant of Him.
But if we die before we have
a chance to merge with Him,
forever may we roam the Wheel
with never chance again,
to live within *the* Temple,

Messages from the Masters

and hear the Master's Call
which frees us from this Netherland
and the dreaded axe of Kal.

Human Birth

© Richard Andrew King

Human birth is critical
to the journey of the soul.
Our actions taken day by day
determine where we go
when the current lifetime ends
and its karmas all wrap up.
Do we descend to deeper depths,
or do we journey Up?

If the Journey can progress,
it can regress as well.
If the soul can rise to Heaven,
it can surely fall to Hell.
If we can take a forward step,
we can, as well, fall back.
How critical is this human birth
to keep us on His Track?

Just because we're human
doesn't mean we gain
a human birth forever,
so we must seek to tame
the impulses and instincts
which trap us in the Wheel,
and keep us from advancing
to Divinity's Ideal.

Messages from the Masters

It won't be long before our days
come, sadly, to an end.
And who knows just how long
the time will be 'til then?
Tomorrow or the next day?
We never know the 'When'
of the Reaper's Deadly coming
when he wields his scythe again.

Therefore, it is critical
for us to mind the store,
for the actions that we make today
may bind us evermore
to life upon the Wheel
and rounds of living hell,
or life within His Light Domain
where Life is ever Well.

Bibliography: Chapter Five

1   Holy Bible, 1 Corinthians 3:16

2   The Science of the Soul, Maharaj Jagat Singh Ji, Radha Soami Satsang Beas, p. 25

3   Sar Bachan, Huzur Swami Ji Maharaj, RSSB, Book 1, #s19 to 24

4   The Science of the Soul, p. 117

5   Ibid., p. 172

6   Guru Nanak, His Mystic Teachings; Professor J. R. Puri, RSSB, p. 283

7   Ibid., p. 50

8   Bible, 1 Corinthians 3:16

9   Spiritual Gems, Maharaj Sawan Singh Ji, RSSB, L 116

10   The Science of the Soul, p. 107

11   Ibid., p. 170

12   The Science of the Soul, p. 50

13   Ibid., p. 50

14   Ibid. p. 64

15   Sar Bachan, Book 2: Sayings; # 215

16   Ibid., Book 1, # 31

17   The Science of the Soul, p. 64

18   Kabir The Great Mystic, Isaac A. Ezekiel, RSSB, 4th edition, 1979, p. 113

19   Ibid., pp 125-126

20   Spiritual Gems, L 129

21   Ibid., L 175

22   Ibid., L 33

23   Guru Nanak, His Mystic Teachings, p. 50

24   Webster's New Collegiate Dictionary, G. & C. Merriam Company, 1977

25   Bible, 1 Corinthians 6:19

26   Ibid., 11 Corinthians 6:16

27   The Science of the Soul, p. 63

28   Ibid., p. 73

29   Sar Bachan, Book 2, Sayings, # 236

30   Bible, St. Luke, 11:37

31   The Science of the Soul, p. 27

32   Bible. St. John, 14:6

33   The Science of the Soul, p. 65

34   Ibid., p. 75

35   Sar Bachan, Book 2: Sayings, # 83,

36   Ibid., # 86

Chapter Six

REINCARNATION

Reincarnation is a fact.
It is part of the Creator's scheme.[1]

T o *incarnate* means to *take a form, a body*. To *reincarnate* simply means to *take it again.* The principle of *reincarnation* says that, as souls, we live through the experience and process of continually *incarnating*, that is, continually *taking on a form or body* as we live through the experiences of our existence in this creation.

Eastern philosophy, religion and mysticism have long understood the reality of this principle. As Perfect Mystic, Master Sawan Singh Ji, has stated: *reincarnation is a fact. It is part of the Creator's scheme.* In other words, the process of continually incarnating or taking on new forms and bodies is the reality of our existence - at least in this dimension, this creation - as we move from life to life.

Western philosophy has not as yet fully embraced this factual principle of life. But in its defense it is still relatively young and unknowing. Western religion currently seems to disclaim the principle of reincarnation. Why is perplexing. Western religion is, for the most part, founded on the teaching of Jesus, but it cannot be overlooked that Jesus was an *Eastern Mystic*, not a Western one. Jesus was born, bred, schooled and taught in the *East*. His teachings are purely *Eastern* in nature. If one studies *Eastern* thought, one cannot read the Bible without realizing its rich *Eastern* heritage and legacy and corroborating the fact that Jesus' teachings, in fact his whole life and life style, were *founded in Eastern thought, philosophy, understanding, precept and principle.* To deny this concept is impossible. Christ was not born in New York, St. Louis, Chicago, Los Angeles, San Francisco or Omaha. In fact, these cities, obviously, did not even exist at the time. Christ was born in Bethlehem of Judea, i.e. in the *East*, to the parents of Mary and Joseph, the later being the son of David, in the family line of Abraham. Clearly, an *Eastern* lineage.

Why this explanation of Western and Eastern thought of Jesus Christ? Because current Western thought, by not understanding the principle of reincarnation and, in many cases, decrying and denouncing it, is prohibiting souls now incarnated in the West from realizing their full and complete spiritual potential. To understand *reincarnation*, its functional operating law - *karma*, and its foundational structure - *transmigration*, is an absolute *must* for any soul seeking true Spiritual Salvation and Liberation.

Again, why? Because by understanding the spiritual-cosmic reality of how this creation functions, one can make better choices bearing directly on his or her spiritual evolution. Understanding this triadic structure of *reincarnation, karma* and *transmigration* is unequivocally critical to one's spiritual choice-making process. Success in anything rests on sound judgment and the clear, sagacious assessment of fact which generates sound, clear and sagacious action. Wrong information, incorrect information factored into the decision-making process, will yield disastrous consequences. So it is for the soul and its spiritual evolution. Spiritually wrong information, incorrect information, however heartfelt or sincere, will still yield untoward consequences for the soul. It is critical to have correct data to make critically correct choices, and nothing is more critical to the soul than its eternal well-being. Thus, it is crucial to understand *reincarnation, karma* and *transmigration* because a lack of understanding of these factual spiritual principles, as well as a lack of applying them to daily life, will only lead to severe and disastrous consequences for the soul.

When these concepts are universally understood and accepted, perhaps the world will be able to dissolve the polarized concept of *Western* and *Eastern* spiritual thought. Fact is fact. The triadic principle of *reincarnation, karma* and *transmigration* need have no labels, either Eastern or Western. Spiritual truth is spiritual truth. Labels are unnecessary and tend to cloud, distort and obfuscate reality, making spiritual reality confusing. But it need not be. *Personal experience* via *direct perception*, not intellect, is the basis for Truth, and all spiritual Masters base their teachings on *personal experience* of the Divine, not on intellect.[2] This is why Maharaj Sawan Singh Ji is able to affirm: *Reincarnation is a fact. It is part of the Creator's scheme.*

Paramount to this issue of spiritual well-being is a second fact. Spiritual Salvation - the release of the soul from the clutches of this dimension and re-establishment in its true Home with God - occurs *during life*, not afterwards. In other words, Salvation after death does not exist. Salvation occurs within the process of living, *now*, while in the human body. *Reliance on Salvation after death is the finest form of self-deception man practices on himself. If there is no Salvation while alive, it will not come after death. He who is illiterate when alive cannot be a scholar after death.*[3]

How can one argue with this logic? If one wants to become a concert pianist, one doesn't wish or hope or pray to be so, go to bed one night and wake up the next morning playing with the skill and beauty of an accomplished pianist. It's foolish to think that wish-fulfillment produces results. Results require work, effort, training, study, practice and more practice *in the present*. So it is with spiritual development. It is not a matter of foolish, ignorant and immature wish-fulfillment. It is a matter of work, effort, training, study, practice and more practice *now. . . in the present*. No one waits until death to become a pianist, artist, doctor, lawyer, teacher, engineer, athlete, musician, contractor, etc. One does it when alive, when *living* in the *ever-present present*.

Understanding reincarnation, karma and transmigration allow one the necessary background to get on with his or her spiritual training and development *now, in the present*, in the day to day activity of *this life's* experience. Everything is accomplished in the all-pervasive *now*. Thinking that anything will be accomplished tomorrow, the next day, the next year or after death is utterly incorrect. Spiritual attainment is accomplished *now, within the presence of this human body and its life time*, not later. Therefore, each of us is spiritually admonished not to wait until death to seek Salvation. Salvation happens *now*, during this very breath, not when the breaths are gone and the soul is detached from its human form.

When we expand this concept, it is not so difficult to understand reincarnation. Everything in the universe has order, structure. If it did not, science could not exist. But science does exist because there is order to all things. Basic physical elements are the same on earth as in other parts of the universe. Hydrogen is hydrogen. Oxygen is oxygen. Helium is helium. Carbon is carbon. The molecular structure of our human skin is the same; our anatomy is the same; the function of our physiological systems is the same. Certainly, and irrefutably, there is order.

However, when we look at the lives of people, they seem to be disordered. Some people are rich. Some are poor. Some are healthy; some sick. Some struggle day and night to make ends meet for their whole lifetime while others do nothing and experience a life full of ease and comfort. Some slave at their jobs only to fail while others succeed with relatively little to no effort. Some are gifted athletes. Some can't seem to keep from stumbling over their own feet. Some are extraordinary musicians and artists. Yet, some couldn't for the life of them play or sing a note or make a meaningful stroke with a brush or pen. If there is order in the universe, why this apparent disorder?

There is no disorder. It is our perception that is incorrect. This creation is based on the principle of Cause and Effect. Scientists understand this. If there were no factual principle of cause and effect, we could not successfully send men into outer space or cure diseases. Every cause has an effect and every effect has its initiating cause.

It is this underlying principle of Cause and Effect that is responsible for one person being born into riches while another is born in poverty; why one enjoys health while another suffers with sickness; why one person, like Beethoven, begins composing music at an extremely young age and another may never sit down at a piano. Beethoven's skill, as the accomplished skill of many individuals coming into this life, is exceptional because it is the *effect* of a prior *cause* of having studied music, most probably in another life or lives. Just as no one goes to bed wishing to be a classical pianist and awakens the next morning being so, likewise, no one dies in one life and reawakens in another life without taking with him attributes, talents and characteristics of the previous life or lives. Beethoven's skill and artistry were merely the effect of studying and being involved with music at an earlier time. His life, as all of our lives, was the result of cause and effect on a macrocosmic level, i.e., life to life, incarnation to incarnation. Thus, there is order in our lives. Nothing happens randomly.

The Bible overflows with this concept of Cause and Effect. Jesus simply called it the Law of Sowing and Reaping - what we sow, we reap. The *Eastern* word for this universal principle is *karma*, the Great Law of Compensation and Adjustment. *Karma* is the basis for reincarnation. Simply, what we sow in one life or lives comes full circle in another life or lives. Perfect Master Maharaj Jagat Singh Ji declares, just as Christ declared:

As ye sow, so shall ye reap.[4] *The law of karma is universal. It is the fixed and immutable law of nature. Each soul must reap what it has sown. Every soul shall have to bear the exact consequences of its actions.*[5] *When death overtakes a man, he is simply transferred or transported to another field of action. That is the sum of it. And his accounts go with him. If their accounts are not settled before death, they simply must return to this world for the settlement. No soul can ever detach itself from its accounts until they are settled.*[6]

This is karmic reality. This is the basis for reincarnation and why each of us keeps coming back into this life. We have created actions, *causes*, and they must, by natural law, have their reactions, *effects*. If we spend time developing musical skills in one life, they may be manifested more fully in another, like Beethoven and Mozart. The same is true for us all. Our actions, behaviors, conducts and desires of one life or lives act as seeds [initiating causes] which must come to fruition as an effect at some other time. That 'other time' is usually in another life at another time, in another incarnation after we have been *reincarnated*.

In fact, Jesus and his disciples had to be intimate with the principle of reincarnation. Once again, in St. Matthew, Chapter 16, verses 13 and 14, we read:

13: *When Jesus came into the coasts of Caesarea Philippi, he asked his disciples, saying, Whom do men say that I am?*

Messages from the Masters

14: *And they said, Some say that thou art John the Baptist; some, Elias; and others Jeremias, or one of the prophets.*

The disciples of Christ could not have answered in this way unless they possessed a working knowledge of reincarnation. Jesus was not shocked to hear such an answer because he understood reincarnation as well. How could he not? He was an *Eastern* mystic. Reincarnation is as much an integral part of *Eastern* thought, philosophy and spiritual teaching as flour and water are to bread. They are inseparable. Surely, says Maharaj Sawan Singh Ji: *Reincarnation is a fact. It is part of the Creator's scheme.*

Jagat Singh comments: *The Law of Karma is a self-operating law of cause and effect. A seed sown must sprout. Whatever you sow now, you will have to reap either in this birth or the next. Every action produces reaction which, in turn, produces further reactions and this vicious circle goes on forever. Every karma originates from desire.*[7]

As we can see, this understanding of karma and reincarnation is powerfully and relevantly critical to our spiritual development and evolution. What we do *now* - the seeds we plant *now* in *this* life, in *this* incarnation - determines what we reap in subsequent lives, in subsequent incarnations. If we can be made ignorant and blind, left in the dark as to the reality of our actions, behaviors, conducts and desires in this life and how they will manifest themselves in subsequent and other lives, we will not be as discerning and carefully critical as to the choices we make *now* in this life and that lack of critical thought, discernment, choice and action will have devastating and irreparable effects at a later time and probably when we least expect it or can least tolerate it.

Spiritually, we cannot allow ourselves the luxury of playing or acting dumb or ignorant in relation to these principles of reincarnation and karma. We need to understand them. And once we truly understand and accept them intellectually, we then need to alter and modify our behaviors and actions to incorporate and embrace them functionally lest we be relegated, even doomed, to suffering the ill-effects of the very effects we caused.

This principle of karma is exceedingly exact. *Not even a single grain that inadvertently enters your granary from a neighbor's field can go unaccounted. You simply must pay for what you get. The law is inviolable and it cannot be set aside. The payment may be either in kind, in coin or by transfer of an equivalent good karma, but payment there must be!*[8] *None,* says Maharaj Jagat Singh, *can escape the result of his deeds. You shall have to reap what you have sown.*[9]

But, of course, somebody will believe he can escape it - this inescapable, inexorable law of karma. In fact, it would seem the entire world believes it can do so because very few people live their lives by its principle.

Messages from the Masters

People create, every second of every day, the most horrible of actions, thinking or not knowing that they will have to suffer from those very actions they create. And it's not as if people don't know. *Eastern* culture is extant with the teachings of Saints who adamantly proclaim this Law of Cause and Effect. *Western* culture lives by science which is built upon the same Law of Cause and Effect, and *Western* religion, which is based primarily in Biblical thought and teaching, clearly espouses the Law of Sowing and Reaping, which is the same law as the Law of Cause and Effect, the Law of Karma. Yet, Perfect Master Maharaj Charan Singh has declared: *Karma - nobody can escape whether one believes it or not.*[10]

As Maharaj Sawan Singh proclaims: *The Karmic Law is inexorable.*[11] The word *inexorable* means *relentless*; *inflexible*; *immovable*. In other words, it's here to stay. It's not going away. It is a design of God Himself and He, the Power of all powers, wants it to be *the* operational basis of this creation. This Great Law favors no one and *operates without regard to persons.*[12] Says Maharaj Charan Singh Ji: *This whole world is a karmic field, and whatever we do, whatever seeds we are sowing, we have to come back to reap the fruit thereof.*[13] Furthermore, he remarks: *Everyone has to pay off his own karmic debt. Neither you are responsible for the other person, nor is he responsible for you. We are each responsible for ourselves.*[14] Harken to this truth brothers and sisters - what we sow, we must reap! It is *the* Law!

In light of this, Great Master continues: *The Karmic Law is supreme and inevitable, and the sooner we reconcile ourselves with it the better.*[15] No one escapes it. But where is the reconciliation? The entire world moves en masse to its own inexorable ignorance of Karmic Law. It cares not one iota about the very law upon which its entire life and well-being are founded. If there were any greater ignorance, any greater foolishness, let it be shown and known. And also let it be shown and known the penalties for ignoring this great and inexorable Law of Karma for they are terrifying!

The Wheel of Transmigration

The third aspect of our triadic spiritual-cosmic construct is *transmigration.* It is as factual a truth in this world as *reincarnation* and *karma.* When one understands its grim and gruesome reality, truly understands it, then, and only then, perhaps one may shudder and shiver in the awareness of the penalties of violating karmic law and thereby set about to revolutionize his life forever through spiritual living.

Transmigration is the migration of the soul through the *Field of Forms.* This *field of forms* contains eight million four hundred thousand species into which the soul may have to incarnate. Called the Wheel of Eighty-Four Lakh Species [one lakh equals 100,000] in mystic literature, it is also known as the Wheel of Eighty-Four, simply the Wheel or, as its Indian name, *Chaurasi*.[16] The breakdown of life forms within this Wheel is as follows:[17]

The Wheel of Eighty-Four

Life type	Number
Man, including other forms of humans, ghosts, angels and quadrupeds	400,000
Life in water	900,000
Birds	1,400,000
Insects	2,700,000
Plants and trees	3,000,000
Total	8,400,000

The germane point here is that each of us, according to Saints, has been transmigrating within this wheel of living species for millions of lives, eons of time since we came into this creation. Rarely do we get the human form, which is the very top of creation. And the great frightening fact of all this is that if we abuse or misuse our human form, our human body, our human experience by not living a spiritually focused life and seeking union with God, we could be thrown back into this wheel. This is more the rule than the exception.

Guru Arjan, one of India's Perfect Masters who lived between 1563-1606, says: *Many lives hast thou passed as insects and moths, many as elephants, fish and deer; for many lives wert thou bird and serpent, and for many horses and trees. Oh seek God now. This is the time of union with the Lord, for after a long time hast thou got the human form.*

This truth is confirmed by Maharaj Jagat Singh: *Family, parents, children, we had in every life. Food, sleep, lust and greed are also common to all forms. The unique quality in human life, which is not present in any other forms, is the capacity for God-realization and permanent release from the prison-house of Chaurasi. This rare privilege is not bestowed upon any other species. This is the time to seek a Master, learn the technique from Him* [of spiritual ascent and God-realization] *and reach our Eternal Home whence we do not return to this world again.*[18]

Swami Ji Maharaj, founder of Sant Mat, exhorts us: *This valuable body you got after roaming in millions of lower lives. Now do not lose it in vain pursuits. Take heed! Give your attention to Devotion* [of the Lord]. *Have pity on your poor soul and save it from transmigration's wheel. These pleasures and comforts are for four days. After that a long period of sorrow awaits you. Beware! Save yourself from hell-fire; do not make your soul its fuel.*[19]

And just in case someone is thinking that it might not be bad to live the life of an animal, fish, bird, insect or plant, Great Master - Maharaj Sawan Singh - has this sobering remark: *What can be said of the lower forms? Their life is simply miserable; and, being devoid of sense, they cannot liberate themselves from birth and death.*[20]

The clear and distinct message from the Masters is that only man is given the rare privilege to realize God, and if he blows it, if he foregoes the opportunity of seeking God in this human form *now*, he will be thrown back into this great wheel of malicious misfortune and have to stay there for millions of lives.

Is this a future any of us want? Is this a risk any of us can afford to take? Are we so ignorant or arrogant we would not believe a holy host of Perfect Saints who declare this truth and who, with one voice, warn us of its dark reality? Are we so insufferably blind we cannot even see a glimmer of truth in the words of these Masters? We believe doctors. We believe teachers. We believe professors, counselors and other professionals. Why do we not believe those souls who are manifestations of God Himself, who come from God to save us from the dark reality of this dimension and the errant ways of our human condition and who are the Spiritual Ph.D.s of the Cosmos? They tell us that *reincarnation, karma* and *transmigration* are all factual realities of this creation and that we'd better wake up to them or suffer the inevitable and dire consequences of violating them.

Top of Creation

These Saints tell us that man is the top, the *very* top, of creation. No other form of living being is equal to man; not even gods, goddesses and angels. Man occupies *the* highest rung on the ladder of creation and to him and him alone is given the incomprehensible gift and opportunity of gaining his release from this sorrowful and tragic environment and returning Home to God.

Let's try to place this in perspective. Picture a ladder. Each rung of this ladder represents one specie, one life form of the eight million four hundred thousand forms existing in the Wheel. And, just for analogy sake, let's say that these rungs are placed only one foot apart. Thus, in simple terms there would be 8,400,000 rungs or 8,400,000 feet of actual ladder. If we divide 8,400,000 feet by 5,280 feet - the number of feet in one mile - we get 1,590.9 miles or in round figures: 1,591.

Now let's place ourselves on the very top rung of this ladder of transmigration. We look down. But 'down' is an extremely l o n g w a y. It is 1,591 miles down! It is so far down we can't even see the bottom. Even in an airplane, we lose sight of human beings, that is we can't distinguish them from an airborne height of only several thousand feet. But 1,591 miles up in the air, looking down! It's a huge distance carrying natural imperceptions.

Then, if we're sentient, we have to consider falling down this ladder of Chaurasi all the way to the bottom, a bottom we can't see from the very top rung, a rung which we currently occupy for a brief time. Were we to fall, the fall would be utterly horrific. What would be left of anyone falling a few feet let alone 1,591 miles? But let's say we do fall and survive it by the grace of God, which is the only way we would survive it. In this descent we would have lost our human consciousness, our intelligence, our ability to think and choose and discern and act in a spiritual capacity. Remember, it is only given to man to realize God. Therefore, he is the only living being among 8,400,000 species who is spiritually endowed.

So, we survive the fall, but. . . in an extremely limited capacity. What's next? Who knows? But the goal now is to make it back up to the top of the ladder, a journey of 1,591 miles! How do we do that when, because of our lack of intelligence, we don't even realize there is a ladder, let alone a top rung of the ladder or that we should climb it, or that there is anything above and beyond it?

Even if we did know of our predicament, the climb would be nearly impossible. Think of the immense difficulty of those who have tried to climb Mount Everest, the highest mountain peak in the world whose summit is in excess of only five miles, not 1,591 miles! Only a few people have made it to the top of Mount

Everest because of its overpowering and treacherous hazards, and many have died trying.

In this regard, what kind of Herculean effort would it take to climb a ladder reaching 1,591 miles high? Who has the desire, dedication, determination, devotion, discipline, strength, stamina, endurance, courage, commitment, energy, concentration, vision and absolute, imperturbable, unyielding, relentless will to make such a monumental, treacherous and hazardous ascent? This from an age where the average person loses all patience and tolerance when he or she is not instantly and comfortably gratified! No wonder Masters tell us that if we lose this human opportunity we won't get it again for millions of years! Just the thought of having to make such a climb would send most souls into dark despair.

And that's the very point. To lose this priceless opportunity of the human form and be thrown back into the Wheel of Transmigration is *the* most dark and despairing of all tragedies. It is no vacation to live within the dismal and shadowy recesses of Chaurasi. *Now*, Saints tell us, we have the chance - the one great golden opportunity to get out of the torturous madness of the Wheel. . . forever! But if we don't wake up to the reality of this transmigratory reality, we have no one to blame but ourselves! Woe be unto us for being so blind, so ignorant, so foolish, so inextricably enamored and enraptured with the pleasures, charms, allurements and sensations of this maya-ridden and conflicted material world that we lose the very opportunity to escape from it, never return to it, and live forever in unspeakable love and bliss in the Palace of the Lord.

Maharaj Jagat Singh declares: *As ye sow, so shall ye reap, and thus goes on the never-ending cycle. Not one life but many lives hast thou had to pass as animals and insects. At the end of each life appear the angels of death who deal the soul an appropriate reward or punishment. The human form is the only privileged one to realize the Supreme Being, and one gets it again after countless ages spent in other forms. Yet, even here, the mind and senses overpower the soul. . . Every time we [mortals] get the gift of a human form, instead of utilizing it for God-realization, we turn to sensual pleasures and once again go down into the labyrinth.*[21] This is the reality of Chaurasi, the Wheel of Transmigration, the Wheel of Hell.

The Whirlpool

If this analogy of the ladder is not potent enough, let's use the analogy of the *whirlpool* which is another appellation for the Wheel of Transmigration. Think of this ominous vortex. It is a whirling and swirling mass of water whose irresistible force sucks anything down into its abysmal core. Man, who is the top of creation, swims at the mouth of this swirling maelstrom. Deep within this core, of course, are 8,399,999 other living forms. During his brief, all too brief placement at the top of this whirlpool so he may have a chance to get a 'breather' from the stagnant air and pitiful life below in the pressured-filled, ice-cold depths of the whirlpool and, more importantly, to be saved by the Master Helmsman of the passing Spiritual Ship of State and save his soul, man spends his time basking in the sun, surfing the powerful waves of the vortex he ignorantly and fatally misunderstands and mistakenly misreads as existing for his pleasure and, thereby, seals his doom.

Having expended his energy in meaningless and ephemeral joys and pursuits at the mouth of the whirlpool, he eventually grows tired, weary and weak. Unable to sustain his stamina, and having squandered his 'time in the sun', he is tragically and all-too-predictably sucked back down into the vicious vortex, never to see the light, fresh air and freedom that he had while being in the human form at the top of the whirlpool again. He was doomed from the very beginning. Not by God. God gave him a choice and chance to get out, to escape forever, but man doomed himself by his insatiable desire to be fulfilled in the temporal pleasures and pursuits of the whirlpool - the wanton, woe-filled whirlpool of this spiritually malignant world.

The Prison

To continue, we can use another analogy, the analogy of a prison, a prison containing 8,400,000 cells. Eternally it seems, the warden of the prison - the negative power - forces us against our will to move from cell to cell within the prison, confined to our limited spaces, walls, bars and obvious condition of non-existent freedom - in other words, slavery and bondage. There is no fresh air in this prison; no contact with positive, spiritual beings because prison is for convicts, souls who have broken the law and must pay for their misdeeds and crimes. The agonizing screams and wails of numberless, tortured souls are deafening. The overwhelming reality of total and absolute confinement is psychologically maddening. The insanity of the situation breeds despair, fear and hopelessness beyond measure.

But one day, the warden, at the behest of the King, moves the soul to the uppermost cell in the prison for *one* day. This cell is like no other. It has windows. There is fresh air. There are amenities and delights not afforded to the countless numbers of other inmates in the cells below. And. . . there is an escape hatch at the top of this cell. Pasted on the walls are directions and instructions of how to make one's way to the escape hatch and be freed from the prison forever. There is even a Good Samaritan who sits by the cell and is ready to help the imprisoned soul to escape, protect him in his jailbreak and guide him Home to freedom.

Unfortunately, the prison warden has filled the cell with such delights and distractions that the prisoner loses sight of the true value of this cell. He is so enamored with his unique surroundings, surroundings he hasn't had since he could remember, that he becomes enveloped by them and their pleasures. The Good Samaritan talks to him and tells him of his great good fortune, but the prisoner pays no heed, so caught up is he in his temporal passions of material exhilarations that he loses his concentration and goes pleasurably deaf, dumb, blind and insane.

Sunset comes. The sun sets. Night arrives again, on schedule. The prison guards, at the instructions of the warden, reclaim the prisoner and send him back down, down into the stench and bondage of the cells below for such a long period of time that the prisoner will forget his experience in the uppermost cell. This pathetic inmate, caught up in his cellular joy, wasted his precious opportunity to escape through the hatch at the top of the Great Cell with the help of the Good Samaritan stationed all the while by his side. Tragically, one more soul of the billions upon billions of souls in the prison, fails to escape from the nightmare which has haunted him for eons, and the great tragedy is that he has no one but himself to blame. He was given the opportunity. He was given the place. He was given the Guide. But, as he had done as others like and before him, he squandered his chance. A slave he was. Tragically, a slave he will remain. Sorrowfully, his epitaph reads: *Here lies one who was given a chance of freedom but chose slavery.*

Summary

Like the prisoner, we are *now*, in this very lifetime, in this very body, being given a chance, the chance of all chances. Saints tell us that the Wheel of Transmigration is very real. Karma is real. Reincarnation is real. Together they form the spiritual-cosmic structure of this creation. *Reincarnation* is the process. *Karma* is the Law on which it is based and *Transmigration* is the structure within which it is housed. We are *all subject to it. No one is exempt.*

Believe not? Maharaj Sawan Singh Ji remarks as to transmigration: *Where lies the difference in the major part of humanity and the animals except in outward forms? Both eat, sleep, fear and reproduce alike. The difference in intellect and reason is only in quantity and not in quality. Man's life work is to find his 'Where' and 'Whence'. And if he has not done that, he will be reborn in the form best suited to his desires. "As you sow, so shall you reap." If man does the actions of animals, why should he not go back to the animal form? After undergoing punishment in the lower forms of life for his actions, he was born as a man. And if he does the actions of animals, he will go back again to that level and suffer.*[22]

How do we escape this certain tragedy? By finding a Perfect Living Saint, a Son of God who has the power to save the soul; then follow his teachings, which are the teachings of all Saints throughout all time, and devote this human birth, this human incarnation, to Devotion of the Lord. To be sure, *all are drifting towards Chaurasi.* Whoever wishes to escape the dreaded terror of the Wheel of Transmigration should practice love and devotion for the Perfect Master of the time. *There is no other way of escape.*[23]

Karma

© Richard Andrew King

With every step we take

let it be known -

we reap the fruit

of all we've sown.

No innocent tear,

no painful cry,

No sad misfortune

strolling by.

We do the act,

we plant the seed;

The *Law* exact,

we reap the deed.

From life to life,

from time to time,

Precise our sentence,

cruel or kind.

No soul escapes,

no soul defies,

We roam the Wheel

for countless lives;

From birth to death,

around we go

in Maze of Maya -

tortured soul;

coming, going,

endless forms,

blinded eye,

countless storms.

Our only grand

and saving grace -

to meet a Master

face to face;

to beg His mercy

for our life,

to end the turmoil

and the strife;

to end the suffering,

nightmare plight;

to bathe us

in resplendent Light;

To free us

from the hell we roam,

to guide, protect and

take us Home.

Incarnation's Game

© Richard Andrew King

Life to life our faces change.
Likewise do our names,
gender, form and personality--
Incarnation's Game.

Craving spawns attachment.
Attachment pulls us back.
We could not be a prisoner
without a sense of lack.

Desires dictate where we go,
in the realms where we'll perform
as man or beast or vegetable--
it's all a Play of Form.

Higher thoughts grant higher forms.
Lower thoughts the same.
Devoid of flaw, designed by Law--
Incarnation's Game.

Bibliography: Chapter Six

1   *Spiritual Gems*, Maharaj Sawan Singh Ji, Radha Swami Satsang Beas, L 115

2   *Guru Nanak, His Mystic Teachings*, Professor J.R. Puri, RSSB, 1982, 2nd edition, p. 49

3   *Spiritual Gems*, L 103

4   *The Science of the Soul*, Maharaj Jagat Singh Ji, RSSB, p. 73

5   Ibid., p. 98

6   *The Path of the Masters*, Dr. Julian P. Johnson, RSSB, 1939, p. 371

7   *The Science of the Soul*, p. 220

8   Ibid., pp. 195-196

9   Ibid., p. 208

10 *The Master Answers*, Maharaj Charan Singh Ji, RSSB, A 472

11 *Spiritual Gems*, L 129

12 Ibid., L 102

13 *The Master Answers*, A 407

14 Ibid., p. 415

15 Ibid., L 38

16 *Spiritual Gems*, p. 391

17 *Radha Swami Teachings*, Professor L. R. Puri, RSSB, 2nd edition, 1972, p. 36

18 *The Science of the Soul*, p. 50

19 Ibid., p. 64

20 *Spiritual Gems*, L 56

21 *The Science of the Soul*, p.73

22 *Spiritual Gems*, L 168

23 *Sar Bachan*, Huzur Swami Ji Maharaj, RSSB, *Book 2 Sayings*, # 178

Chapter Seven

THE WORLD

This world is the lowest and most miserable of all,
but as we go up into higher spiritual regions,
we enjoy more and more happiness and have no
desire to be born into this world again.
Saint Sawan Singh

As seekers of God following a spiritual path, our goal is to return Home to the loving, warm, eternal bliss of the Lord's embrace. How fortunate are we that we should be so inclined to move in such a supernal direction?

How difficult, however, is this journey? We are *all* still here, struggling within the confines of this earth. Why? Perhaps one reason is that we are too tied to this world, too enjoying and being enraptured by the passing parade hosted by the Prince of Darkness who is himself the parade's Grand Marshall. We are, it would seem, inextricably caught in the devil's lair - a dark, dank, dung-steeped, maya-ridden morass which is so

Timeless Truths for Spiritual Seekers   King

perniciously intricate, nefariously complex and hopelessly inescapable for the majority of mankind that Guru Nanak remarked: *How completely helpless mere men are!*[1] Fortunately, however, as seekers of the Truth we have chosen to follow the Path, to purify ourselves, pay our debts, burn off our karmas and balance the books so we will one day, through the Master's promise, leave this pleasure-saturated, pain-filled, pejorative prison house and dungeon of darkness and return Home.

Perhaps though, in the quest to hasten our liberation and motivate us to be disciplined and enthusiastically committed to our meditation - the real work of our lives - it would be good to take a closer look at *this* world which has been described by Maharaj Sawan Singh Ji as a dung heap, a cesspool, a latrine, and which Huzur Maharaj Charan Singh has further described as a *dark and filthy dungeon into which the Father has sent me.* Lovingly, however, he reassures us by promising, *I will also draw you out of this dark dungeon back up to the Father as soon as you have been cleared of all your Karmas or sins.*[2]

What Is This World?

What is this world? Great Master says in Spiritual Gems: *The world is the design of Kal and Maya, the negative forces.*[3] *The world is a plaything of Kal.*[4] Emphatically, he declares: *This world, with all its attachments, is nothing but a deception practiced by*

Kal.[5]   Kal, of course, is the great negative power who manages *this* creation, and in these previous quotes Great Master is elucidating the clear fact that *this* creation, *this* world in which we live, is totally ruled by the Devil himself.   Satan, of course, is not an equal power of God, but he is the house manager so to speak, the warden of this nether prison.   As seekers of the Truth, we should have absolutely no allegiance to him whatsoever or to this realm which he governs.   As we are blessed with the omnipotent Master's protective shield, we have absolutely no commitment, no devotion, no loyalty nor fidelity, not only to the negative power but to *this* world as well.   Yet, we must still live here until the final and auspicious moment of our destined release.

The question therefore arises, "Because we are *spiritual* seekers, why do we give this creation so much attention?"   We are, after all, *still* here.   Is this not because our consciousness is still soaked and saturated with the world's passing pleasures, amusements, allurements and charms?   Are we not doing our devotional work, our meditation? This nefarious black pit in which we move and live and breath and dwell from minute to minute, day to day, hour to hour, week to week, month to month, year to year, decade to decade, life to life, and which we have regarded as home, is not our true Home. As Swami Ji says: *This world, which is a wilderness, has been mistaken for a residence.*[6]

Additionally, he says: *The world is perishable and so are all worldly things. The wise man is he who realizes the transitory and illusory nature of this world and all things pertaining to it and makes the best use of this body by worshipping the Supreme Being through Bhajan and Simran.*[7]

Guru Nanak, the most famous of the ten Sikh gurus and whose writings compose the first part of the Granth Sahib declares: *The world is bound in cords of attachment and much hope; only the teaching of the Guru gives a sense of detachment.*[8] Furthermore, he observes: *The entire world is within death's compass. Without the guru there is no means to conquer it. Who are imbued with Truth are saved; they dispel doubt and duality.*[9] Poignantly, Nanak continues, *in the web of its own actions is the whole world caught and it does not realize it.*[10]

The "Cobbler Saint" Guru Ravidas states, *This world is a house of collyrium [an abode of evil]; a veritable well of the poison of egotism.*[11] Moreover, he remarks: *This world is a field of suffering which is known to all. The wise man reaps his harvest with God's Name while the fool, weeping, reaps it in tears.*[12]

Kabir, the "Weaver Saint" born to Muslim parents and a contemporary of both Guru Nanak and Ravidas, exasperatingly comments: *The world is blind, engulfed in utter darkness, but to whom can I explain this?*[13] *Such is the world*, says Kabir, *it is led away by nonsense, but when it hears of the Path of Truth, it rejects it as false.*[14]   And furthermore, *The whole world is in misery in a greater or lesser degree. . .only he is happy who has conquered his mind through the Guru's grace.*[15]

Huzur Swami Ji's Master, Tulsi Sahib, the Saint of Hathras, tells us to, *Look all around; there is nothing of consequence in the world.   This short-lived pageant will be left behind.   Pelf and poverty, kith and kin will be of no avail.   Indeed, O Tulsi, life is as fleeting as the existence of the moth in the flame.   All the world is moving towards death, but none solves the mystery of the end.*[16]

Maharaj Jagat Singh Ji, also known as "Guru Ji", Great Master's successor, heartfully tells us: *Brothers, this world, full of misery and pain, is not thy true Home. Thou belongest to the land of Everlasting Peace and Bliss where there is not grief, disease or death.   These religions are not thy religions, nor are these castes thy castes.   Thy religion is love.   Thy caste is Sat Nam, thy country is Satlok or Sach Khand.   Thou art the son of the Father - the True, Eternal, Unborn, Deathless, without Beginning and without End, [Father].   Thou hast fallen into the hands of Mind and Maya who have kept thee confined to the wheel of births and deaths.   Human form is the only exit through which thou canst find escape.*[17] He goes on to say, *The world is literally a Pandora's Box - a home of misfortune.   True happiness does not exist anywhere. . . This world is not our true Home.   It has nothing to offer but pain and sorrow. Quit this place as soon as possible and reach your True Home in Sat Lok without delay. Take heed! This work can be accomplished only in the human form. Therefore, take full advantage of this opportunity for it is the greatest good fortune to be born as a human being after long and tortuous wanderings in other lives. You have a short span of life and this, too, is running out fast. Unless you wake up now, it will be futile to cry over split milk later.*[18] *There is nothing but utter darkness and misery in this world. It is, indeed, a place where the blind are leading the blind.*[19]

Therefore, given these clear, precise and direct comments from God Himself through the guise of these Perfect Living Masters, why have we not yet awakened from our deep sleep? As Huzur Maharaj Charan Singh Ji asked just before he left the body, *Why are you still here?* Even the Old English poet Geoffrey Chaucer, author of the Canterbury Tales, but no where near being a mystic of the highest order, declared in his poem, "Ballade of Good Counsel:" *Here is no home. Here is wilderness.* It doesn't take a Saint, therefore, to see the reality of this world. It is not a paradise. It is not our home. Home is inward and upward.

Worldly People

As spiritual seekers of the Truth, we are in the process of ascent, of climbing the divine ladder of salvation. Our roots to *this* world are in the process of being severed, destroyed. It's just a matter of time before we're done here. It is only a matter of time before our worldly consciousness withers, dries and dies. Therefore, to aid the process of our transition from this world to His World, we need to be careful and cautious of the time and attention we give to this worldly environment and its people. We are going Home, "Home" with a capital 'H'. This 'Home' is our true residence, our true domicile, our true and eternal place of rest. But we cannot go until our worldliness is dissolved and destroyed, until there is not even a nano shred of it (the world and its consciousness) left in our being. As long as our conscious is still rooted here, we are worldly people, and even though we may be spiritual beings having a human experience, the higher experience, the ultimate experience, is to be spiritual beings *living* a spiritual experience. That we can only have when we reside in the higher realms of Love, Life and Light. Until then, we cannot afford the luxury of thinking of ourselves as more than we are. We're *still* here. That means our consciousness is *still* here. Our attention is *still* here. And to be sure, we have to work hard to get out of *here*.

Yet, for those who are genuine seekers, the divine promise is that we're to leave *here* one day. So there exists in us at the present time this dichotomy wherein we find ourselves being in the world yet trying to get out of it. We may be spiritual beings having a human experience but, as aforementioned, the ultimate is to be spiritual beings *living* a spiritual experience. Thus, even though we're looking forward to being in His realms of resplendent light, we cannot be arrogant in the thought that we are different from other people in the world. After all, He made us all and, after all, we are all *still* here!

Saints talk at length about worldly people. And since we're to leave the world one day, we must be acutely discerning of the worldliness in others as well as ourselves in order to guard against the nefarious and evil traps set by the negative power, for, as we remember, this world is his domain and we can ill-afford to don the blinders of myopia and amblyopia (short-sightedness and dim-sightedness). We must be able to see clearly and not be fooled, for this world *is* a wicked place. *And God saw that the wickedness of man was great in the earth, and that every imagination of the thoughts of his heart was only evil continually* (Genesis 6:5). In fact, the word *wicked* is used no less than four hundred ninety four times in the Bible alone, not to mention its plethoric use by saints throughout the ages. All one has to do to confirm this is think of the billions of animals slaughtered every year on this earth just to satisfy the insatiable palates of those who choose to devour their flesh. At any level, slaughtering life is an indefensible and heinous act of barbarism, an incomprehensible and unconscionable act to an enlightened consciousness. Who is man to take the life, any life, of any creature that God creates and to whom He gives life? Only God has a right to take what is His. Such arrogance of killing for his own pleasure compounds the wickedness of man. And then there is man's greed, his lust for power, riches, sensuality; his anger and all of the destruction, turmoil, tears, fears and chaos it creates, not to mention the endless catalogue of ills caused by man's ego. Need more be said? Killing, lying, deceiving, cheating, stealing - these are all egregiously wicked acts defining man, defining us as worldly people. They do not speak well for our spiritual enlightenment. If we open our eyes just a wee bit, we cannot help but understand this truth. Make no mistake, this world is a wicked place. It is no home, and it surely is not Home.

Our ultimate goal as divine seekers of the light is to live in the presence of God Himself. *Evil* is *live* spelled backwards. Thus, as long as we remain here, we are existing in a backwards state, moving and breathing in direct opposition and antithesis to God's Way and His Divine life style.

Maharaj Charan Singh Ji says: *People of the world are interested only in talking of worldly things.*[20] *They do not realize that no matter how great the pleasures of the world may be, they are not only short-lived but also have equally unpleasant reactions at some time or another.*[21] *Worldly people only love those who are attached to the world so it is useless to expect them to love you.*[22] *Worldly people. . . cannot even bear the sight of anyone who tries to open their eyes and shake them loose from all these chains that bind them to the world so they persecute and malign the very person who is trying to help them while they honor, flatter and worship those who put more and stronger chains on them to bind them still tighter to this world.*[23]

In talking of worldly-minded people, he further questions, *How can you even think of God when you are steeped in flattery and worldly personalities? The honor that you give one another is false and meaningless. Real honor comes from God and that we can get only when we honor the Son of the Father and through him go back to our true Home.*[24] Therefore, in loving reassurance he says, *Do not worry about public opinion and the criticism you get from worldly people because you are on the path. . . Every lover of the Lord has to face criticism and sometimes even persecution at the hands of the world.*[25] And, to his disciples he reaffirms: *You do not belong to this world. By the Grace of the Father I have chosen to take you out of this world so naturally the worldly people hate you.*[26]

Guru Ji, Maharaj Jagat Singh, tells us, *The view of worldly-minded people about the success and failure of life is utterly wrong and misleading. Their aims and objects are limited to the gains and pleasures of this world only. They do not understand the immense value of human life on this plane nor its purpose and goal. We should pay no heed to their opinions. They do not realize that the sole object of human life here is to 'go in' and make contact with the Inner Master and the Sound Current so as to get release from the cycle of births and deaths to which we have been subject ever since the world was made.*[27] In fact, he says, *Regarding worldly relationship, it may be pointed out that all relationships are based on selfish motives on this material plane. Husbands, brothers, wives, sisters, other relatives and friends are attached to us because of the advantages that accrue to them from us and are apt to cool down in their zeal and love towards us when they feel that we are of no use to them. Do not expect much from them but do your duty towards them and care for them even if they fail to reciprocate your love.*[28] Furthermore, Guru Ji states, *All worldly people are prisoners awaiting the stroke of death, save for that rare brave who hath his body in prison but his soul in heaven.*[29]

Tulsi Sahib, in his poem 'The Vain Pursuit,' declares, *People toil in pursuit of worldly desires; who cares for the search of Truth? They relish the pleasures of their senses and revel in their passions. . . They attain not salvation while living but babble about attaining liberation after death.*[30]

In speaking of worldly-minded people, Great Master states, *The friend of this world is the Manmukh (devotee of the mind). . . Burning with the worldly passions he comes and burning with them he goes. Having entangled himself in sensual pleasures by following the dictates of his own mind, at the time of death, the messenger of death takes him away. And after examination by the Dharam Rai (King-Judge), he is placed in hell. This is the fruit of the friendship of this world.*[31]

Kabir remarks: *Strange are the ways of people. They are like flocks of sheep. If one falls in a ditch, then all the others, instead of learning from experience, throw themselves in it too without a thought.*[32] Continuing speaking of worldly people he says: *You lead, in this low world, the life of a beast since you remember not the ever-present Lord. You do not know the True Name of the Lord, so in the end, the ashes of your flesh will fall into your mouth and pride will vanish without allowing time for your repentance.*[33] Emphatically, Kabir warns: *Serious seekers must avoid the company of the worldly minded however good they may be otherwise.*[34] *Keep not the company of one with divided mind. He hopes to serve the Lord but he is merged in the world. Keep away from one not attached to the Merciful; push him off with both thy arms.*[35] And, in speaking of domestic ties, he admonishes us, *Give up all pride of family and pedigree and attach yourself to the True Name of the Lord; thus you will save all of your family. He who is attached to Nam* (the Divine Word of God) *and detached from his family renders the highest service to all his relatives.*[36]

Guru Nanak says: *The ignorant worldling cherishes not his Lord, but cries out to Him when overcome by suffering. The pain and pleasure we experience are the result of our past deeds and He, the giver, who has bestowed them on us, alone knows. O man, whom, then, can you blame? You reap whatever you yourself have sown.*[37] Adamantly, Nanak exhorts us to: *Remember the Lord, brothers. This is the way all must go. Transient are the attachments of this world; certain is the journey henceforward.*[38]

Perhaps some of the most stinging, but nonetheless loving admonishments, come from Saint Kabir. He states: *Listen, dear seeker. A day will come when you will have to pass from here leaving behind even the loin cloth covering your nakedness. Of what value are all thy worldly desires?*[39] *Keep thou the company of Saints. For even if on dry bread you must live, that company is still more precious than aught else. Evil alone springs from the worldly people's company.*[40] *I tell thee again, remember the Name, else after death thou shalt repent and then it shall be too late.*[41] And in regards to the entire spectrum of soul liberation and Divine Union, Kabir's scalpel of Truth cuts most surgically when he declares: *What can the ignorant know of the bliss of God-realization? What can they know, these worldly fools; these fools, fools, fools?*[42]

Foolery

Why are worldly people so foolish? Isn't Kabir being somewhat harsh when he so boldly calls people of the world fools? When the entire purpose of human life, the *only* true and lasting purpose, is to become realized in the pristine purity of His Love and Spirit, and when beings of this creation, age after age, form after form, life after life, incarnation after incarnation, birth-death and rebirth after birth-death and rebirth keep playing in and on the dunghill of this world oblivious to the true reality of their human form when they acquire it and then proceed to waste it by squandering it in worldly pursuits and ignoring the reality of His Great Message of God-realization, is this not being foolish? Yea, is this not being the supreme fool? Perhaps Kabir is being kind and gentle by simply and lightly calling people fools. People of the world could be called a lot worse. But, as Maharaj Charan Singh Ji remarks: *Saints never criticize or condemn anybody. They do, however, call a spade a spade. They give out pure truth.*[43] Thus, for a Saint such as Kabir to call worldly people fools is not disparaging. It is simply the truth. Spades are spades and fools are fools, and those who choose to wile away their precious human birth in pursuits other than the quest for God-realization cannot be named otherwise.

And for each of us, as a spiritual seeker of Truth, are we also not playing the fool by ignoring our responsibility and duty to turn away from the world and concentrate our attention on Him who is gracing us with the priceless and exceedingly rare gift of the human form and its opportunity of soul liberation from the incarcerating bondage of the Wheel? Is there no greater fool than one who knows the truth but who refuses to act on what he knows, or who makes a promise, a deal, a commitment and refuses to keep up his end of the bargain; who is oh-so-willing to receive but not to give or give back? As easy as it would be to consider ourselves 'holier than thou' because we have been blessed with the thought of spiritual enlightenment, are we not the greatest of fools if we refuse to acknowledge Him and His great gift while we not only live in a human body, which He gave us freely, but also ignore the edicts of His commands and our commitment to Him to be a genuine follower of the Path? Perhaps some honest reflection on our own foolery is appropriate and meaningful.

Worldly Fools At Large

This worldly foolishness is readily apparent for instance in the propensity of humans to slaughter, kill, destroy and eat the flesh of other creatures. Since time immemorial, Saints have warned against this heinous and vile act, yet few heed their warnings. Says Guru Nanak: *Countless are the cutthroats who trade in violence; countless are the sinners who thrive on sin and evil; countless are the impious who live on unwholesome food.*[44]   *In the web of its own actions is the whole world caught and it does not realize it.*[45]

Guru Ravidas is emphatically frank and direct about the eating of meat. He says: *Those who eat meat, they, in fact, get their own throats cut. For whosoever is a meat-eater, he will have to go to hell. Having no sense of compassion in their heart, they eat the flesh of another. They are bound to go to hell, truly does Ravidas declare. He who ever eats cows and goats for the sake of nourishing his body, he can never go to heaven even if he offers holy prayers day and night. He who eats meat and fish for the sake of pleasing his palate, he will have his own head severed in return for causing death unnecessarily to a creature.*[46]

Tulsi Sahib, the great Saint of Hathras, is equally direct in calling a spade a spade. He says: *They verily fall into the dungeon of hell who slaughter living beings and eat their flesh. . . For the sake of sensual gratification they buy sin and get their abode in the fires of hell. Whoever has eaten flesh and fish in this life is bound in captivity by the butcher, Kal. Nothing good will come out of such conduct. Take this as evidence from the writings of Saints. Nanak and Kabir have given the same message; Dadu and Dariya have sung the same song. Tulsi declares from the housetops: kill not the living; within all resides the beloved Lord - listen, O men and women!*[47]

Messages from the Masters

Eating the flesh of other creatures is not the only path to worldly foolishness. Through the path of learning and intellectualism one can equally miss the spiritual mark. Says Kabir: *How can you explain the knowledge of realization to the learned? Kabir is hesitant even to try to explain inner experiences for they are non-understandable. What is the use of dancing before the blind? The art is wasted. The intellectual has no regard for the Master. He doubts all things that you explain; he accepts nothing. The senses have gripped him tightly in their fast grip and he is destined certainly for hell. Realization is no matter for discussion. It is a practical, yet mystical attainment. And every intellectual I have seen has ever groped in doubt about the spiritual truths. No intellectual is certain or can ever be.*[48] He goes on to say: *Learning makes thee in all truth a heartless stone and writing makes thee just a veritable brick, for Love Divine has not by these methods entered thy heart. Love is not born of books. They only tend to make thee stony-hearted.*[49]

Swami Ji corroborates Kabir's words. He states: *Learned and clever persons are not fit for the society of a Sat Guru* (the supreme spiritual teacher) *because they are filled with conceit and will not believe in the Sant Sat Guru. Saints give out what They have seen, but these ignorant persons depend on what they hear or read and wish to prove things by the force of intellect.*[50] *Saints and pundits have never agreed nor will they because pundits advocate external forms of worship while Saints insist upon internal devotion.*[51]

Beyond intellectualism, the world's understanding of religion also bars us from true spiritual knowledge because Satan misleads us by making us worship dead, not living, Saints.[52] In this regard Swami Ji declares: *In short, it is impossible for anyone to attain salvation by simply believing in or worshipping a Saint, prophet, incarnation or god who lived in the past.*[53]

And then there is the worldly-religious and foolish promise of salvation after death. Maharaj Sawan Singh Ji comments: *Reliance on Salvation after death is the finest form of self-deception man practices on himself. If there is no Salvation while alive, it will not come after death. He who is illiterate when alive cannot be a scholar after death.*[54] Guru Ji further illustrates this point by saying: *A thief who has lived on theft the whole of his life cannot be a saint after death. Death is only the giving up of the outer covering of the material body. In all other respects one remains the same. So try to get Salvation now while living.*[55]

This false promise of a peaceful, wonderful, glorious life in heaven gained after completion of a life wasted in worldly pursuits while in the human form is further exposed in the book *Kabir The Great Mystic* by Isaac A. Ezekiel. We read: *All Saints are emphatic about the terrors of death. . . Not only is the hour of death often an hour of terror, but the hope of peace and repose thereafter is founded on imagination. Troubles of the physical body may end, but the astral and other bodies still continue with us. Mystics like Kabir explain that we have been born thousands of times; we have died thousands of times, and we will have to be born and die thousands of times more unless, of course, we come to the feet of a Perfect Master. . . At the time of death, the astral body, the causal body, the mind and the soul are dragged out of the physical body in which they are enmeshed.*[56] Death is an extremely painful, not pleasant, experience: *The pain of death is so acute that it is equivalent to being stung simultaneously by a hundred thousand scorpions* (Philosophy of the Masters, Volume I, p. 100). Therefore, to avoid this most unpleasant occurrence, finding a Living Master, asking for Initiation and following his instructions are most critical for the journey beyond.

In reference to death, some people who have had out-of-body experiences (mistaking such occurrences for death) say they do not fear death. This statement is in contradistinction to that of Saints who say that death is filled with immense terror and pain. So . . . whom does one believe? One would be wise to believe Saints and not be fooled by statements to the contrary. Why? Because people who have had out-of-body experiences did not actually die. They may have honestly thought they died, and they may have been given a glimpse of the astral region (the next spiritual level up) and its light

194

(which is one thousand times brighter than our physical world), and this more than likely prompted their comments about having died not being afraid of death, but they could not have factually died.

The fact is, having an out-of-body experience and dying are two different things. In an out-of-body state there is a separation of the consciousness from the body but not a severing of the life force from the body. There is, Saints tell us, a *silver cord* that attaches the soul and the body, and unless this *silver cord* is cut, there is no death. Says Sawan Singh: *There is a silver cord by means of which one can leave the body and return to it at will and be at all times connected with it. In this manner he gets an insight into death while living. He travels in the astral, the causal and the higher regions and becomes fully familiar with them. He is able to meet and talk with the inhabitants of these regions* (Philosophy of the Masters, Volume I, p. 103).

However, when this cord is severed, one cannot return to the body and death occurs. Therefore, people who have experienced out-of-body states did not really die. They simply had an out-of-body experience. But die? No. Had they died, they would not have been able to return. Therefore, their understanding of death and their point of view in not being afraid of death, is fallacious and misleading.

Masters bring a different message of death. Sawan Singh comments: *Death is merely the withdrawal of the*

Messages from the Masters

soul from its gross coverings and its entrance into finer regions. It is merely giving up the present garment, namely, the body. It does not mean annihilation. There is life after death, although we may not be able to see it. Charan Singh adds: *Life does not begin with birth and end with death. We are an expression of infinite life which had no beginning and shall never come to an end.* Saint Dadu states: *Some say one can secure abode in paradise after death. They, indeed, are making the world insane.* Tulsi Sahib corroborates this message: *Those who give assurance of salvation only after death are cheats and charlatans. Who has come after death to give evidence that he has attained deliverance? The true path is that which gives salvation in his life, and while living. The incarnations come to destroy the evil-doers, not the evil in them. The Saints, ever loving and merciful, come to emancipate sinners, not to kill them.*

Another issue of concern is that of worldly power, wealth, status and position. How many worldly people, nay, how many of us, have been made fools by falling into these traps? For those who seek power through rulership, Maharaj Jagat Singh Ji reminds us of Shakespeare's *Henry IV, Part II*: *Uneasy lies the head that wears a crown.*[57] Guru Nanak further reiterates this point of worldly status and station by declaring, *Ranks of this world will not be recognized in the next; none knows what will befall him there. Remember the Lord brothers. This is the way all must go.*[58] Tulsi Sahib states: *Thou hast amassed and accumulated much in this world, but a day will come when all thy possessions will perish. With such a rare incarnation thou hast become swollen-headed; after a while thou shalt be called to face justice. Body, mind and wealth will be of no avail; they are all empty and hollow like leather bellows. Leave the changing colors of this petty world, says Tulsi. The Lord's Name alone is the true wealth.*[59] Of worldly riches Guru Ji declares: *The poorest man in the world is he who has nothing but money.*[60] In fact, Baba Jaimal Singh admonishes us to *Look upon money as the dirt of your hands.*[61] Finally, Great Master encapsulates the entire foolish activity of amassing worldly wealth and riches into just five words: *Golden fetters are also fetters.*[62] In other words, chains of gold are still chains and no matter how rich a person is, that person is still bound and tied to this wicked world.

And what of worldly merry-making, parties and good times? Simply, such activities gain us nothing. Says Kabir: *Throughout your life your thoughts have been of nothing but eating, drinking and of making merry, but you forgot completely your Earnest Friend, the True Name of the Master.*[63] As Huzur Maharaj Charan Singh Ji points out: *The purpose of our coming into this world is not merely to eat food. The real purpose for which we were created is to worship the Father and merge back into Him, and we cannot achieve that purpose unless we are on the Path.*[64]

Messages from the Masters

In relation to the sense enjoyments of the world, Professor Jagat Singh remarks, *The sensual world is indifferent to the fate of the soul. Despite the misery it goes through, it still clings firmly to the momentary pleasures.*[65] *All form, beauty and fascination of the world is nothing but illusion. It is a well-designed net that ensnares us all. The five passions - lust, anger, avarice, attachment and pride - are commissioned by the Negative Power to mislead both mind and soul and make trouble for them.*[66] Interestingly, *Satan has especially appointed angels whose prime responsibility is to prevent our spiritual progress and lure us to squander our spiritual wealth.*[67] It is all so foolishly worthless. As Swami Ji declares: *All worldly pleasures are a source of pain and eventually will betray their possessors.*[68] And, to set the party issue straight, Kabir tersely proclaims, *God does not make love with women.*[69] By this comment he is saying that sexual indulgence for either males or females is deleterious to spiritual devotion. Saints are not singling out females. They often use the word "woman" or "women" in referring to sex lust in both genders.

Dealing with the World

So how do we deal with the world? We have to live in it after all. Maharaj Charan Singh Ji tells us: *We have to die now as far as the world is concerned and to live as far as the Lord is concerned.*[70] *We cannot reform this world, and this world will never become a heaven, but will remain at daggers drawn and there always will be killing in this world. Saints do not come to reform this world. They just come to take us away from this world.*[71] *There will never be peace in the world; there never was peace in the world. As long as the mind is there, human conflict will remain the same. . . The purpose of Saints is to take us away. We are all prisoners here.*[72] And how do we deal with worldly people? Maharaj Ji simply says, *We should not be drawn towards the worldly people. They should be drawn towards us.*[73] In other words, he or she who is devoted to the spirit should not be magnetized to any worldly personage.

Maharaj Jagat Singh Ji gives us this advice: *You are to live in the world but in a sensible way. Enjoy the world and its objects but realize their true worth. They are meant to serve you. Take full service from them but do not yourself become their slave. Let not your mind become so entangled in attachment to these objects that, instead of being of service to you, they become your master. . . Live in the world but be of God and not of the world. . . Enter this garden of the world. Take a walk in it. Enjoy the fragrance of the flowers. Eat fruits and behold the beauties of Nature, but do not get entangled in thorns and prickly shrubs lest you may get abrasions and wounds. . . Earn wealth honestly and spend it well. It is meant for you. Attend to your work during the day. Day is for work. But at night give some time to devotion and contemplation. This is your 'real work'. . . which will, in due course, liberate you from this vast prison in which you have been confined for countless ages.*[74]

Perhaps the most succinct advice comes from Baba Jaimal Singh. He suggests, *You should live in this world like a duck which, though it lives all day in the water, flies with its wings quite dry.*[75]

Summary

In summary, we can reiterate the position of various Saints regarding this world. Guru Ravidas states: *A dense forest of poisonous trees is this world. Many are the miseries, conflicts and calamities in it. Men desirous of enjoying its beauty rush to it as moths to the flame. The affliction of lust is the foremost trap of the world. None so entrapped has ever attained the Truth. Why shouldst thou be delighted and comforted in it?*[76] *Harken, O mind. The day of death is at hand and yet thou hast not disowned the mesh of the world!. . . Every moment death is tightening its grip on thy soul and yet thou does not wake up.*[77] *The ocean of the world is extremely dreadful. Why dost thou not understand this, O foolish one? Know that Nam* (the Word of God) *is the boat and the Guru is the rudder thereof, sayeth Ravidas.*[78]

Guru Nanak comments: *The entire world is within death's compass. Without the Guru there is no means to conquer it. Who are imbued with Truth are saved. They dispel doubt and duality. Only those the guru protects are saved. The worldling is born only to die and be born again. Ask the Guru for knowledge and seek the company of Saints. If the mind is imbued with God, one comes not nor goes. There is no deed better than practice of the Lord's Name.*[79]

Kabir says: *I saw an ant carrying a grain of rice and then she spied a grain of pulse [seed]. She was puzzled how to carry both. Kabir says, she cannot. She must take the one and leave the other. So must a devotee choose between the Lord and the world.*[80] *How strange it is that no one seems to care about their future which is Everlasting Life. Remember, you will leave here empty-handed for you can carry nothing with you in the worlds beyond. All who are born must die.*[81] *I must never forget that none's my true companion here, for all are gathered here for selfish ends. But the foolish mind can never understand this, cannot believe that this is all illusion.*[82] *This worldly life lasts only for two days. Be not entrapped in it. Attach yourself to the feet of the Perfect Master for there alone you will get eternal bliss.*[83]

Tulsi Sahib exhorts: *Kal hath put the world in distress, O friend. Go thou beyond his realm to reach*

Messages from the Masters

thy True Home.[84]   Swami Ji Maharaj relates: *The soul is surrounded by enemies. No one is its friend. Even the mind. . . watches the spirit just as a cat does a mouse which it intends to devour. All beings here are unhappy for Kal inflicts suffering even on his own souls - that is, those who follow him and obey the dictates of the mind. But the souls of a Sat Guru have always His mercy upon them and even Kal is afraid of them and helps them. It, therefore, behooves all of us to take refuge in the Sat Guru of the time. This would insure safety and protection both here and beyond.*[85]

Great Master declares: *The governance of this world is in the hands of Kal and he has so arranged that no soul should go beyond his sphere.*[86] *This material plane on which we function is of the lowest order and, in comparison to this, the astral and causal planes are much superior. . . The delights of the spiritual planes above the Causal are infinitely greater than what one is familiar with on the lower planes.*[87] *The whole world is asleep as far as the centers above the eyes are concerned.*[88] [The world] *is to be dissolved and her people also.*[89] Continuing he says, *The world has nothing higher to offer than the Truth* (of the teaching of the Saints).[90] *We must turn from the world and obey with love and faith the instructions of the Master.*[91]

Rumi, a Muslim Saint of Persia, also known as Maulana Rum, says, *This world is a prison and we are all prisoners in it. Break through the roof of thy cell and release thyself.* [92]

And, finally, perhaps the most succinct and direct message of all regarding living in this world is from Maharaj Charan Singh Ji who says so simply and beautifully, yet clearly, distinctly and commandingly: *Just live in the creation and get out of it!* [93]

The World of Fools

© Richard Andrew King

In this loveless land of Spirit lost
where the Prince of Darkness rules,
there stands a sign before the gate,
"Behold! The World of Fools!"
Ignorance and insanity
reign supreme within this land.
For eons struggles every soul
to reach the rung of man,
and when God finally lifts the soul
to the highest rung within the Wheel –
eight million four hundred thousand rungs –
man forgets to kneel!
He takes his form for granted,
squanders priceless time,
wastes his every precious breath
to rise above the Mind;
above, beyond this evil land
where Satan, truly, rules;
thus hangs a sign around his neck –
"Behold! The Fool of Fools!"
Caught in senses and in pride,
attachment, lust and greed,
man falls, again, sadly again
for the signs he did not read.
"You do not own your body,"

says the Lord to lucky man.

"I've graced you with this *human* form

so you can leave this land

and rise within My Kingdom

to come and be with Me,

to live within My warm embrace

for all eternity;

to share the peace, the bliss, the love –

as all souls with Me feel;

and all I asked was your sweet love,

but you forgot to kneel.

Instead, you lost yourself in sin.

You, My commandments cherished not.

Somehow, you never realized

that with a price you're bought!

This human body is not yours.

I gave it you to see

if you would love the world

or give your love to me.

Sadly, you have missed the chance

to use this holy tool

to finally gain Salvation,

and, *still*, you play the fool!

Have you never heard My Words?

Do you scripture never read?

Have you no knowledge of the Law?

Why do you never heed

the teachings of the Saints

Messages from the Masters

whom I gave to judge the world,

to lift you *in* and *up* and

prevent you being hurled

back into the Wheel

where fears and tears abound,

where eons you will wail and flail,

where I can ne'r be found,

where you will howl in horror,

drenched in demon fright,

for failing, while in human form,

to seek My Living Light

and live within My Sacred Laws,

laws based in purity?

In truth, it is the *only* way

to avoid this tragedy.

I have told you very clear –

you rest in *My* employ,

and if you violate *My* Laws

you I will destroy!

Your body *is* the Temple

of the Living Lord of Light,

and if you choose defilement,

then I will set you right,

and I will throw you back

into the fire 'til you learn

that you must not defile me

or I will make you burn,

burn not to destroy

Timeless Truths for Spiritual Seekers   King

but to purify your mind

that you finally learn to cherish

this *human* life Divine.

Please do not be deceived.

I have made My Laws.

If you choose not to honor them,

your tears will have their cause.

I will not tolerate your sin

in this *human* form I gave.

Repent and purify, my love,

or your soul I will not save.

Listen not to earthly talk,

or those from worldly schools.

This land is not My Paradise –

it is My World of Fools.

God and Mammon you can't serve.

Divided houses fall.

One day you'll be made to claim

the consequences of your call,

and if you lead a holy life,

all will turn out well;

but if you don't then, tragically,

I will send you to hell,

and you will burn, make no mistake,

for eons, fire and strife.

So critical is this *human* form,

so priceless is *this* life,

that if it has been wasted

Messages from the Masters

and focused on the world,

back into the endless depths

will your soul be hurled.

Beware! I warn you! Heed these words!

The end *is* coming soon.

Do not squander this great gift

and lose this precious boon.

The time is *now* to seek the Lord.

Wait not another day.

Endless darkness waits for thee

if you choose not to pay

the price for loving God

and seeking all that's pure,

for cherishing this *human* life

and to the end endure.

Please, dear child, time is near

when Death *will* wield his tool.

Purify your life in Mine

and do not die a fool!"

The Land of Strangers

© Richard Andrew King

I live in a land of strangers,
isolated and alone,
where no one speaks of Spirit
or mentions going Home;
where no one seems concerned
with their life beyond their death;
where earthly pleasures saturate
and consume their every breath;
where killing and consuming flesh
are status quo to most,
and sexual symbolism is a goal
and crown of which to boast;
where celebration takes the form
of crude, unholy ways,
and worldly accomplishments
are heralded with praise;
where alcohol, intoxicants
are ingested as if food,
and all that is promoted
is vicious, dark and lewd;
where all that's pure and virtuous
is mocked and jeered with glee;
where men have no awareness
of the cost of being free;
where men give little value

Messages from the Masters

to their priceless human form

and its golden opportunity

from the moment they were born;

where having sense of consequence

is deemed a human flaw;

where blindly men keep falling

in ignorance of the Law;

where fear of one's own actions

is met with pure disdain,

and success is based on money

and wealth of earthly gain;

where the honor of one's word

is displaced to what is writ;

where men reject all effort

requiring a little grit;

where straight talk's substituted

for that which curves and bends;

where getting to the bottom line

is where attention wends;

where man seeks woman, woman, man;

where few men seek the Lord;

where fools are tools and tools are fools

until the cutting of the Cord

when all is lost and squandered

and pride becomes regret,

and laughter turns to misery

with realization of the debt

that never was discharged

Timeless Truths for Spiritual Seekers   King

when the chance was well at hand,

when man had opportunity

to be a stranger to this land,

and move on in and up

to regions filled with Light,

where peace and bliss and love prevail

in ignorance of the night;

where knowledge of the pain

and sorrow of the heart,

have no validation

to one not set apart

from God and His Pure Kingdom

where souls roam ever free,

illuminating wondrous Light

beyond Eternity.

Yes, I live in a land of strangers,

temporarily, until when

He makes me whole and lifts my soul

forever back to Him!

Until that time I wait,

impatiently, I must say,

but, nonetheless, there's knowledge

that there will be a day

when He fulfills His Promise

to rescue wayward souls

from the depths of utter darkness

where the wind of fire blows

Messages from the Masters

ever hot and constant,

unrelenting in its wind

to chasten, clean and purify

until the memory of Him

makes the soul burn hotter

than the wind upon its face,

to realize the value

of the Lord and His great Grace

in liberating tearful man

from the bondage of his sin,

and allowing him another chance

to find the Lord again.

And, thus, I wait, as all souls wait

who live as strangers in this land,

for the Lord to cast the Magic

of His omnipotent Hand

over all of those who suffer

and yearn to be with Him,

who daily pray in solitude

to return to Him again,

and live within His Kingdom

where peace and love abound,

where the lonely word of 'stranger'

can never e'er be found.

Between Two Worlds

© Richard Andrew King

Between two worlds I live, I die;
One below, the other High;
One by instinct, one by soul;
I cling to one but must
Unto the other go.

Eons of habit form my mind.
I cling to that which makes me blind.
But yet, within, I feel the Pull –
The Higher one will make me full.
But yet, again, I cannot leave;
Between two worlds, I cry, I grieve.

I pray to Him to set me straight,
To loose the lock, unlatch the gate;
To cut the cord that binds me so,
To let me to the Higher world go;
To free me from these chains in Pind,
And ride upon the Inner Wind.

'Tis not with ease to change the tide
Of worldly love on which I ride.
Impressions set from eons past,
Cast their net and hold me fast.
Hopeless, helpless, hapless me,
Between two worlds in misery.

Messages from the Masters

The Higher pulls from higher sky;
A future life awaits on high.
The Lower holds with anchor strong,
Memories held too dear, too long.
I want to fly but stuck, I stand,
Prisoner in a foreign land.

Like barnacle to rock I cling,
A prisoner to sensual feeling.
All I've had and all I've known
Has been this rock of maya stone.
Now, from High this feeling comes
Creating consciousness of maelstrom.

With arms upstretched I beg for Light
While sobbing in the dark of night.
Sitting, sitting, sitting still
I cannot seem to crack the Til.
No ease, no peace, no joy of heart;
Between two worlds I'm torn apart.

The race, once started, must be won;
No question of a setting sun.
It is the Dawn of Inner Light
That drives the hope to shed the night.
Yet, still enshrouded by veil dark,
My arrows fly but miss their mark.

Timeless Truths for Spiritual Seekers   King

Between two worlds the battle flares,

Slippery footing on the stairs

Makes climbing higher full of fright;

Deadly falls from higher height,

Have claimed the lives of climbers high;

No room for error or errant sigh.

To claim one world o'er the next

Relieves the stress of come betwixt.

No enviable place to be between,

Convergent waters of polar streams;

To opposite ends dual power flows;

Up-down, up-down, the battle goes.

The Lower World breathes no Soul,

No love, no light, no virtue whole.

Mind runs rampant through flaccid fields;

Deceitful dacoits and passions steal

The very life that seeks to live,

But birth and death are all it gives.

The Higher World resounds with God,

But few are they who this way trod.

Yet promises of Saints declare

Eternal life for those who dare

To climb the mount and fight the fight,

And slay the powers of the night.

Messages from the Masters

Tis no sweet thing to wage this war,
Of different worlds with different shores;
Especially since the one to leave
Contains the history of that we breathe;
But that which holds eternal cheer,
Is the Higher one with promise dear.

Thus, choices made, I lift the bow;
Pull the string and loose the arrow.
'Tis hope divine it finds its mark,
Igniting within eternal spark;
Lighting the way through darkest night,
To pierce the veil and be the Light.

Dear God, please this wayward sinner hear.
Remove this filthy garb I wear.
Clean me, scrub me, make me right;
Fill my heart with Master Light.
Release me from these fields I roam.
Grant me Grace and take me Home.

Let me merge myself in You.
Discard all that is untrue.
Take this drop of ocean mine
And mix it with your Soul Divine.
I plead, I beg upon my knees--
Save this sinner . . . please.

Timeless Truths for Spiritual Seekers   King

Bibliography: Chapter Seven

1   *Guru Nanak, His Mystic Teachings*, J.R. Puri, Radha Soami Satsang Beas, 2nd edition, 1982, p. 35

2   *St. John: The Great Mystic*, Maharaj Charan Singh Ji, RSSB, 4th edition, 1978, p. 128

3   *Spiritual Gems*, Maharaj Sawan Singh Ji, RSSB; Letter 23

4   Ibid., L 115

5   Ibid., L 172

6   *Sar Bachan, Book 2: Sayings*; Huzur Swami Ji Maharaj; RSSB; L 19

7   Ibid., *Book 1: Teachings*; opening thesis statement

8   *Guru Nanak, His Mystic Teachings*; J. R. Puri; RSSB; 2nd Edition, 1982; p. 342.

9   Ibid.; pp. 357-359

10   Ibid.; p. 104

11   *Guru Ravidas: Life and Teachings*; K. N. Upadhyaya; RSSB; 1st Edition; 1982; p. 184

12   Ibid.; p. 150

13   *Kabir The Great Mystic*; Isaac A. Ezekiel; RSSB; 4th edition; 1979; p. 102/103

14   Ibid.; p. 50

15   Ibid., p. 29

16   *Tulsi Sahib, Saint of Hathras*; J. R. Puri/V. K. Sethi; RSSB; 1981; p. 44

17   *The Science of the Soul*; Maharaj Jagat Singh Ji; RSSB; p. 61

18   Ibid.; p. 63

19   Ibid.; p. 69

20   *St. John, The Great Mystic*; p. 24

21   Ibid., p. 61

22   Ibid. p. 136

23   Ibid., p. 143

24   Ibid., p. 46

25   Ibid., p. 135

26   Ibid., p. 136

27   *The Science of the Soul*, p. 158

28   Ibid., p. 135

29   Ibid., p. 110

30   Tulsi Sahib, Saint of Harris, p. 54

31   *Spiritual Gems*, p. 160

32   Kabir The Great Mystic, p. 363

33   Ibid., p. 404

34   Ibid., p. 376

35   Ibid., p. 371

36   Ibid., p. 407

Messages from the Masters

37   *Guru Nanak, His Mystic Teachings*, p. 404-406
38   Ibid., pp. 39/40
39   *Kabir The Great Mystic*, p. 113
40   Ibid. p. 315
41   Ibid., p. 257
42   Ibid., p. 113
43   Ibid., p. 44
44   *Guru Nanak, His Mystic Teachings*, p. 102
45   Ibid., p. 104
46   *Guru Ravidas: Life and Teachings*, pp. 194/195
47   *Tulsi Sahib, Saint of Hathras*, pp. 67/68
48   *Kabir, The Great Mystic*, pp. 392/393
49   Ibid., p. 389
50   *Sar Bachan*, # 19
51   Ibid., # 216
52   *Kabir The Great Mystic*, p. 172
53   *Sar Bachan*, # 52
54   *Spiritual Gems*, L 3 103
55   *The Science of the Soul*, p. 222
56   *Kabir The Great Mystic*, pp. 252/253
57   *The Science of the Soul*, p. 69
58   *Guru Nanak, His Mystic Teachings*, pp. 39/40
59   *Tulsi Sahib, Saint of Hathras*, p. 100
60   *The Science of the Soul*, p. 70
61   *Spiritual Letters*, L # 70
62   *Spiritual Gems*, L # 102
63   *Kabir The Great Mystic*, p. 404
64   *St. John - The Great Mystic*
65   *The Science of the Soul*, p. 109
66   Ibid., p. 104
67   *Kabir The Great Mystic*, p. 129
68   *Sar Bachan*, # 147
69   *Kabir The Great Mystic*, p. 238
70   *The Master Answers*, Maharaj Charan Singh Ji, RSSB, A # 19
71   Ibid., A. 471
72   Ibid., A. 274
73   Ibid., A 550
74   *The Science of the Soul*, pp. 83/84
75   *Spiritual Letters*, L # 100
76   *Guru Ravidas: Life and Teachings*, p. 176
77   Ibid., p. 82
78   Ibid., p. 64
79   *Guru Nanak, His Mystic Teachings*, pp. 357/359
80   *Kabir The Great Mystic*, p. 371
81   Ibid., p. 349
82   Ibid., p. 407

83   Ibid., p. 404
84   *Tulsi Sahib, Saint of Hathras*, p. 59
85   *Sar Bachan*, # 154
86   *Spiritual Gems*, L # 199
87   Ibid., L # 183
88   Ibid., L # 164
89   Ibid., L # 160
90   Ibid., L # 134
91   Ibid., L # 166
92   *The Science of the Soul*, p. 61
93   *Satsang*, Huzur Maharaj Charan Singh Ji, December 2 & 3, 1986 [audio tapes]

Chapter Eight

THE NEGATIVE POWER

Kal hath put the world in distress, O friend.
Go thou beyond his realm to reach thy True Home.[1]

He has been called by many names: the Devil, Satan, Lucifer, the Prince of Darkness, Beelzebub, Dharam Rai and Mammon. Regardless of name, his power is real. He is real - make no mistake about it because to make such a mistake would be the gravest of mistakes. He governs all in this creation because this is *his* creation, *his* world. He spreads a net of illusion, darkness, deceit and ignorance so inextricable that few escape his overpowering grasp. He is our greatest enemy, our greatest adversary. He is the Governor, the Lord of this realm and all of us save only those protected by a Perfect Master are his puppet slaves. He is Kal, the Negative Power.

To understand the Negative Power it is important

that we first gain a brief understanding of the cosmology of the universe as described by Perfect Saints, then all fits into place and we gain an accurate picture of this light-bearing deceiver and entrapper of souls. However, just as certain as he exists, just as certain as his evil is a fact, it is also a fact that God created him and he does God's bidding. God is, after all, *the* Creator of the Universe. None stands against His Word. He is omnipotent, all-powerful, and as Guru Nanak states when speaking of God's omnipotence, *Even the ruthless Kal is only a morsel of His.*[2] Still, Kal has his place in the grand scheme of things.

God's creation is composed of varying levels, grades, planes, dimensions, regions, zones, universes and worlds. Everything that exists was created by God and He is the Supreme Ruler of All. But everything that exists does not exist on the same plane nor at the same level of consciousness. From the bottom up there is an ascending order to God's Divine Cosmos; a descending order if one is looking down from above. Just as in school there are varying levels of education and educational reality from pre-school through college and beyond, so in the realm of the spirit there are also varying levels of spiritual education and divine reality. All this is contained in what mystics call the Grand Hierarchy.

This divinely superb hierarchy is an enormous structure of lords, rulers, creators and governors who preside over the four grand divisions of creation and their subdivisions. Within each subdivision of each major division there are varying spheres or planes each with their own ruler. These rulers, lords and governors are great souls who have been appointed by the Supreme One to discharge the duties assigned to them in their respective regions. They are each endowed with certain godlike powers and prerogatives. At the very top, of course, is God who rules from the Positive Pole. At the very bottom of this hierarchy is the Negative Pole, that region farthest from the Positive Pole, i.e. God's Uppermost Kingdom of inexplicable Light and Love. The Negative Pole is the nether region of creation and is the one in which we reside. It was created and is ruled by the Negative Power - Satan, Kal, the Devil.[3] But ultimately, however, it was created by the Will of God for nothing happens without His Order.

To keep us clear-headed regarding this issue, Maharaj Charan Singh states: *This is all God's creation. In order to run a universe, He needs all sorts of forces to keep people here. If Kal had not been here, we would all have gone back to the Lord again. This universe would not have existed. . . If He does not want this universe, it cannot exist even for a day. It is here because He wants it to be here, and whatever you see has come from Him. Kal is just the administrator of the universe. Kal sees to it that we do not get out of it, that is all. . . He is not without purpose. He is not without the Will of the Lord.*

He is there through the Will of the Lord. Nothing exists without the Will of the Lord. Kal does not derive his power from anywhere else.[4]

Thus, we see that the Devil, Satan, Kal is not, as many religious beliefs would purport, an equal power with God. The Negative Power is, frankly, a lowly subordinate to the Supreme Lord. He's an administrator, that's all, albeit a ruthless and cruel one from whom our job is to escape. Yet, he holds such a low position in the Grand Hierarchy that Guru Nanak has commented that he is only a *morsel* of God. *Morsels* are hardly equal powers.

Dr. Julian Johnson, a devout theologian and outstanding surgeon who traveled to India to teach the gospel of Jesus Christ but who, instead, became a devout disciple of the spiritual path of Living Saints, gives us this description of Kal, the Prince of Darkness, in his landmark book, <u>The Path of the Masters</u>: *The Negative Power refers to that individual in the Grand Hierarchy who occupies the position of Creator and Governor nearest to the negative pole of creation. He is not the lowest in the Hierarchy. Under him are many subordinates. But of all the negative powers, he is supreme. The rest may be called his agents and subordinates. They carry on under his orders, just as he carries on under the orders of his superiors. His name is Kal Niranjan, and his headquarters lie at the summit of Triloki, commonly called the Three Worlds, that is, the physical universe, Anda, and the lower end of Brahmanda [designated as Trikuti or Brahm Lok]* [5]

In the meantime, while we sojourn in this dark region of matter, we have to deal with the Negative Power. With him we must contend in our struggles for spiritual freedom. It is his duty to try to hold us here, while it is our duty to try to escape. The resulting struggle purges us and makes us strong, and fits us for our homeward journey. This everlasting fight, this struggle in a welter of pain and blood and heart cries, is designed by the Supreme Father to purge us and make us clean, ready for our homeward ascent. Let us never become discouraged. All of this is designed by the Father for our benefit. It is much as if one enters a gymnasium to take exercise. If we meet these difficulties in the right spirit, we shall greatly profit by them. The idea of pain and struggle is to purge us and inspire in us a longing to rise above the regions of pain and shadow.

At the present time we are sojourners in the country of the Negative Power and our first duty is to find our way back to our own home. While here, we are subject to the laws of this country. It is to these laws of the Negative Power that we refer when we speak of the laws of Nature. He [the Negative Power] is the author of all natural laws as we know them, for he is the creator and lord of the physical universe. He is the Lord God of the Bible, the Jehovah of the Jews and Christians, the Allah of the Mohammedans. He is the Brahm of the

Vedantists, the god of practically all religions. None but the Saints and their students know of any other god; yet this Negative Power, so exalted and so universally worshipped as the supreme Lord God is, in fact, only a subordinate power in the Grand Hierarchy of the universe. He is the Negative Power, and as such he must have some negative qualities. Of course, when compared with man, he is very exalted, full of light, goodness, wisdom and power. It is only when compared with the Positive Power that his lesser light becomes manifest. To this very fact we may trace the origin of what we call evil; for evil is but a lesser good.[6]

As Dr. Johnson states, the Negative Power is *very exalted, full of light, goodness, wisdom and power.* The Devil does not really run around in a red suit carrying a pitch fork and donning pointed ears and a long tail. We must remember that one of his names is Lucifer. Lucifer means 'light bearing; a morning star'. He is quite beautiful to look upon because of this light, and it is because of his extreme radiance that he is mistaken for God, but he is not God. As far as man is concerned with his limited degree of light, goodness and wisdom, the Negative Power may, with his comparatively advanced level of light, goodness and wisdom, appear to be God, but it is *only an appearance* and one which portends fatal results for one who is so deceived.

Thus, a large part of the modus operandi of the Kal is to make people believe that he, the Negative Power, is

God, the Positive Power, and that his level of being and existence is the absolute highest level. But Saints tell us this just is not so. There are many levels far beyond the realm of Kal, regions from which he is excluded. These regions are known to Masters because they have traveled through these inner spiritual regions and, by *direct experience*, know the truth. However, most others do not. Those who have made it from the physical realm to the astral region see the brilliant light of that next higher level and think this is heaven and God's residence because, by comparison, it is resplendently magnificent, a thousand times brighter than our physical, material universe. True, it is a heaven but not the ultimate Heaven, nor the Supreme Lord's residence. In the Grand Hierarchy there are higher levels and higher orders of Gods, higher degrees of light, love and wisdom, but the Negative Power does not want anyone to know this, and, in fact, he and his minions *do not wish any soul to contact a Sat Guru* [a Perfect Master] *who can deliver that soul from the regions of the Negative Power. He* [Satan] *wishes to keep every one here.*[7] He wishes to keep them here so he has souls over whom he can rule; so he has a kingdom to govern. An empty kingdom - empty of souls - has no value, no meaning to a ruler bent on ruling. Kal's desire is to rule and, thus, he allows for this great deceit to exist and, in fact, has no other choice. His job is to keep souls here until God calls them Home.

Thus, the Negative Power uses whatever is necessary to do his duty.

Let it be said that, certainly, the Negative Power is more advanced than mere men but that does not make him God. It makes him a more advanced being than man. Yet, in spite of his advancement, he has his place and can rise no higher in the Grand Hierarchy. Disciples of Perfect Masters, in fact, by the Grace of the Master, rise far higher than Kal is capable of rising. Disciples of Perfect Masters return all the way Home. This gift is not given to the Negative Power. How precious, then, is being a disciple of a Living Saint?

However, Kal does have great power in relation to us and our perceptions. He is, after all, the ruler of this creation consisting of the entire physical universe and extending upward to the second spiritual region known as Trikuti or Brahm. However, he does not use this power for anything else but to enslave. Maharaj Jagat Singh explains this and adds: *The Negative Power, which governs our world and the regions up to Brahm, is a cruel magistrate who punishes us for our past deeds whether we know their nature or not.*[8] In other words, Kal does not rule by grace or love but by pure, unalloyed justice - an eye for an eye. This is why he has been referred to as ruthless. It also raises the question of karma, the pure law of an eye for an eye.

In relation to this Dr. Johnson states: *Kal is the lord of Karma for this world and all regions up to the second*

- Trikuti. Karma is administered by him to the great bulk of humanity. In fact, in case of all who have no Guru, they follow the routine outlined above, and karma holds sway over their lives from age to age. From the wheel of karmic destiny there is no escape except when one meets a living Master. But the very moment a person takes Nam from a Guru, that is, becomes a disciple, all his karmic accounts are transferred to the Guru's keeping, automatically passing from the hand of the Negative Power. After that, the Guru, working under the directions of the Supreme Positive Power, administers the karma of his disciple. From that hour forward, Kal, or the Negative Power, has nothing to do with his accounts and has no power or control over him. The agents of death cannot approach him, nor can he ever be called into the courts of the Dharam Rai [the Great Judge] *for judgment. His destiny in this life and in the next rests entirely in the hands of his Guru. The Master then administers the karma of his disciple just as he thinks best for the disciple.*[9]

Again, how precious and fortuitous is it to have a Master! Without one all of us are doomed to living in this negative, nether land and being enslaved by its negative ruler. This is why Kabir has said: *Live in this dread world but keep your mind attached to that high world which lies beyond the range and rule of Kal.*[10] Guru Nanak declares: *Kal does not spare those who do not have the support of the Guru. Kal traps us through our eyes and tongue. . . Kal cannot slay if the true One dwells in our heart and we sing His praises. Through the Guru we merge in the Word.*[11] Time and time again Saints extol the absolute virtue of having, following and obeying the dictates of a Perfect Master. Such an enlightened soul saves us from Kal and the Wheel of Transmigration.

Upon this issue Maharaj Charan Singh remarks: *Those who do not meet a Perfect Master or Saint are indeed most unfortunate. They always remain under the sway of Kal, the Negative Power. They have to undergo repeated births and deaths and endure much suffering and misery. They may even have to incarnate as worms. Those who do not find or seek a perfect Master can never contact Nam and according to their karmas will move from one body to another of the prison of this world undergoing untold misery all the time. Relatively, in fact, when they are in this world they are really more dead than alive. Guru Nanak says: He who does not serve the Guru, and does not love the Name of God, should not be looked upon as a living human being, for he is truly God-forsaken and his soul is dead.*[12]

Because the Master is such an intrinsically vital part of the soul's escape from the region of the Negative Power, and because Satan does not want even a single soul to escape, he [Satan] deceives souls. Says Charan Singh: *Sometimes Kal, the Negative Power, assumes the form of the Master or makes you believe that you are in*

Messages from the Masters

the presence of the Lord. On such occasions, or whenever any form comes before you or you hear any voice, repeat the Holy Names. If the form remains, then it is the Master. Other forms, which are deceiving, will immediately disappear. No evil or anti power can stand before the Holy Names. Always make sure by means of this test.[13]

When souls are initiated onto the Spiritual Path of the Masters, they are given specific Holy Names which serve as their shield and support in their journey through the inner spiritual regions. It is these Holy Names, held privately by disciples of Saints, to which Charan Singh refers. He continues: *No entity or evil spirit can do any harm to a Satsangi* [a disciple of a Perfect Master]. *When Kal, their chief, cannot come near a Satsangi, how can his imps touch one?*[14]

Here, again, we see the immense value of placing oneself in the presence and under the jurisdiction of a Perfect Saint. Not only does he guide and enlighten the person, he protects him to such a degree that the Negative Power - Kal, Satan, the Devil - is absolutely helpless to harm him. Even Christ mentions this aspect of having a Master in St. Luke: 18-20. He states: *Behold, I give unto you power to tread on serpents and scorpions and over all the power of the enemy, and nothing shall by any means hurt you.*

Still, some people become afraid of the Negative Power. In a letter to one such disciple Charan Singh states: *Your fear of meeting Kal, which you say comes only at night, is simply childish. It is due to the lack of clear thinking. Kal does not appear at random and to everybody. When and if he appears, by that time the disciple also has gathered sufficient power to smash his head. Please cast out these silly notions from your mind and always be brave. No harm can come to one who is under the protection of a True Master.*[15] The key sentence here, of course, is: *No harm can come to one who is under the protection of a True Master.*

Huzur Swami Ji Maharaj, Founder of *Sant Mat*, the *Teachings of the Saints* (now the *Science of the Soul*), comments on this issue of the Negative Power and his prey. He says: *The soul is surrounded by enemies. No one is its friend. Even the mind . . . watches the spirit just as a cat does a mouse which it intends to devour. All beings here are unhappy, for Kal inflicts suffering even on his own souls - that is, those who follow him and obey the dictates of the mind. But the souls of a Sat Guru have always His mercy upon them and even Kal is afraid of them and helps them. It, therefore, behooves all of us to take refuge in the Sat Guru of the time. This would insure safety and protection both here and beyond.*[16]

Still, a spiritual seeker and disciple must ever be on guard and ever vigilant. As Charan Singh remarks: *When a soul is seriously and sincerely keen to find the Truth, the Tempter [Kal, the Negative Power] tries to mislead it in many ways. Please beware of that.*[17]   This Perfect Master further states: *There are many worlds and regions under the domination of Kal [Satan] to which he would be only too glad to take anyone; more so an Initiate or one who is destined to be initiated. But now he finds that you* [a seeker] *have seriously started on the journey Home, he will try to put as many obstacles in your way as possible.*

He goes on to explain by example. *The owner of a horse leaves it to move about freely as long as it is grazing within an enclosure, the gate to which is tightly closed. But as soon as he finds that the gate has been opened by somebody, he instantly puts a lock on the legs of the animal or takes other measures to stop it from straying out. Similarly, Kal does not bother as long as a soul is confined within the regions under this control. It may ascend to any heights within that sphere. But when he finds that a soul has found the way to its True Home and is intent upon getting out of his Prison-House, he leaves no stone unturned to stop its exit. From the moment of Initiation the real fight has begun. Fight manfully and bravely. . . You will conquer, and Kal will be thoroughly vanquished. The Master is always with you to guide and protect you, so let not despair or despondency come near you.*[18]

Here we again see the Master's reassuring love, reemphasizing that the disciple will succeed in his quest for God-Realization and the Negative Power is helpless to thwart such activity. *You will conquer, and Kal will be thoroughly vanquished. The Master is always with you to guide and protect you, so let not despair or despondency come near you.*

In the preceding passage Charan Singh refers to the domain of Kal as a Prison-House. Saints often use this analogy to describe our helpless, enslaved incarceration in this creation. Dr. L. R. Puri in his book <u>Mysticism, The Spiritual Path</u>, elaborates upon this dungeon-like concept. He remarks: *This whole universe of ours, which is the world of Kal, is a big prison which has many rooms and cells in it. The master of the prison is Kal and we are all prisoners. . . Now Kal does not want that we should go out of his prison back Home although he desires perpetual reform going on within his prison. To that end he sends Incarnations, Prophets and moral, social and political Reformers who all try to set his world right. But they are the agents of Kal and act with his power and do his work of reform within the prison. They do not tell us of our real Home in the Absolute; they hardly know of it themselves. Shabd Mystics on the other hand come from outside the prison and liberate us from Kal's thralldom for good. It is with their help and grace that we go out of delusion and darkness forever and reach our true Home.*

To understand this simile thoroughly, we must know what the various rooms in the prison are. They are the multifarious kinds of life we see in this universe of Kal.

Messages from the Masters

Some lives are bad and wretched like those of beasts of burden, low insects and others animals which are represented in the prison by dark cells and dungeons where people are given hard labor. Higher kinds of life get different bodies. The body of man is the highest cell - an 'A' class cell which affords him the best comfort in the prison. But such a repose in this 'A' class cell is not forever. The soul will eventually be thrown back into the lower, dirtier cells. Thus, in this vast prison house of the Negative Power, the soul roams from cell to cell without knowing or remembering that its true Home is somewhere else. That somewhere else is the Kingdom of the Lord. But this cycle of endless rotation, of transmigration, continues unceasingly in the dominions of Kal, and there is no true peace here.[19]

However, it is the duty of the Negative Power to keep this world in a livable condition. When things become too bad, he sends elevated beings with the appropriate amount of love and wisdom to keep his world in check. These are what are referred to as Incarnations and Prophets. Says Professor Puri: *Incarnations and Prophets serve the purposes of Kal, the master of the prison. They come from age to age to reform lower cells, and take these prisoners into higher rooms; but their reform is internal and within the prison. They do not set us free. We are deceived by them for we think that they come to take us to our Father in the highest realm beyond good and evil which is our Home,*

Timeless Truths for Spiritual Seekers   King

but they keep us within the prison. In fact, Incarnations and Prophets do their work of reform in the prison as state-officials; they move about with decorum. They come to promote good and root out evil; their sphere of activity is within Relativity and Delusion.[20]

Thus, not all reformers come from the region of the Supreme Lord. Many come from the Satan himself. In fact, Kabir, the weaver Saint tells us: *Satan has especially appointed angels whose prime responsibility is to prevent our spiritual progress and lure us to squander our spiritual wealth.*[21] How slick and deceitful are the ways of the Negative Power! It is common thought to regard angels as good, holy, pure, and containing our highest and best spiritual interests in their hearts. Kabir says, 'not so'. There are indeed angels who represent the Negative Power. Perfect Masters alone represent God. This is just one more reason to find a Perfect Saint and follow him. Under his protection one cannot be deceived by such angelic tricks.

Aside from the domain of the Negative Power being a prison, Swami Ji refers to it as a furnace. His description carries ominous foreboding. He comments: *The lure of the world deludes all men, and no one can escape from Kal. The whole world is burning in the blaze of desires; all creatures are tormented in this inferno. No way of escape can be seen, and everyone perforce must burn in this hellish furnace. Day and night this fire consumes them and birth and death they will have to undergo time and again. Thus will they wander about in different bodies without discovering the cure for their disease. How can I put in words the sufferings they undergo? Their misery is indescribable.*[22]

Swami Ji is talking about us, common men and women, as well as all living beings in this creation. To reiterate with emphasis: *Day and night*, he says, *fire consumes them*, i.e., us, *and birth and death they will have to undergo time and again. Thus will they* [we] *wander about in different bodies without discovering the cure for their* [our] *disease. How can I put in words the sufferings they* [we] *undergo? Their* [our] *misery is indescribable.*

This is certainly not a favorable commentary on our lot. In fact, it is quite horrifying. Says the Great Saint of Hathras, Tulsi Sahib: *The ruthless and tyrannical Kal, without the mercy of the Master, is subdued not, so formidable is his power.*[23] As is explained in Guru Nanak, His Mystic Teachings: *The King of Death shows no mercy on sinners.*[24] *Kal spares none who serve not the Guru.*[25] His *messengers of death operate under the orders of their master, the Negative Power, whose duty it is to administer justice with no favoritism.*[26]

Perhaps from these messages it is not so difficult to choose between the only two paths lying before us in this life - the path of the Negative Power with eternal wanderings from form to form within the furnace walls of his dark and dirty dungeon, a slave to his wicked ways of deviled darkness, or the path of the Masters with its assurance of spiritual guidance, protection and God-Realization soaked in eternal peace, bliss and endless joy in the loving embrace of God. There are only two choices. The former leads to incarceration and slavery in hell under the dictates of a cruel magistrate; the second guarantees Spiritual Liberation and Eternal Freedom by being devoted to a Perfect Saint. Which do you choose?

Evil

A discussion of the Negative Power necessitates at least a brief discussion of evil since Satan, the Kal, is generally considered evil. In speaking of evil, Dr. Julian Johnson remarks: *It has no actual existence. It is a lesser light. When light is abundant, there is no shadow; and in absolute darkness, there is no shadow. So it is with evil. The Masters see in evil only a shadow, a state of incompleteness, a phase of growth, perhaps a necessary concomitant of evolution. But in our ignorance, believing the darkness to be something real, we grope about in the shadows. But it is only a negation. The man who never saw light or heard of it would not suspect that he was in darkness. To him that darkness would be normal. So it is with evil. It is only because we know of a greater good that we feel the pain of the evil.*[27]

The man who never saw light is the collective race of beings dwelling in this nether dimension, this dark land ruled by the Prince of Darkness. *The man who never saw light* is us, unless, of course, we are blessed with the spiritual guidance of a Perfect Master who, having seen the Ultimate Light, reveals it to his disciples. Most souls in this world *grope about in the shadows* of ignorance because they have never seen, heard of, listened to or read about the spiritual Truth of the Great Reality of God's creation as revealed by Perfect Saints. This world *is* a dark place, a seemingly evil place because it reflects little light, little love, little spirituality when compared to the higher spiritual regions in God's Kingdom. It is solely a matter of perception, but thank God Saints give us the Divine Perception, the Highest Perception, the Lightest Perception, the True Perception of Reality.

Dr. Johnson continues: *To sum up the entire philosophy of evil, we must conclude that, as a matter of fact, there is no such thing as evil. Evil as a reality is philosophically unthinkable, and there the matter must end so far as metaphysics is concerned. The assumption that evil is a reality has caused much confusion in philosophy and religion. It is of no use to deny the difficulty; we must assume that if evil exists, God is responsible for it. And such an assumption lands us in a maze of philosophical difficulties from which there appears to be no escape. Driven to the wall by this stern fact, many thinkers have declared that there is no God. How can there be a good God in charge of a world full of woe and sin? It is only the illuminating philosophy of the Masters that removes the difficulty. In a universe created by an all-wise God, whose fundamental essence is goodness and love, there is no room for such a thing as evil. It simply does not exist. But there are many degrees of good, of the light. In its final aspect, there is nothing bad in the world, neither is there sin nor fault in anyone. What appears so is due to our limited understanding.*[28]

Thus, in a nutshell, evil is the absence of good, or, a lesser good. It is darkness devoid of light. If we enter a dark room, we may think the darkness is real. But as soon as we turn on a light, the darkness disappears. It does so because it has no intrinsic substance of its own. Depending upon the amount of existing light, there may be shadows in the room. However, as soon as the room is flooded with light from all angles, all shadows, all darkness, disappear. It is also interesting that we can turn light on with the flip of a switch but we cannot turn darkness on because darkness is nothing save the absence of light. It is no thing. Nothing. It is unreal. So it is with evil. It is nothing, no thing, save the absence of light, and the light to extinguish the darkness of our world, of our consciousness, is carried and brought to us in the form of Perfect Living Masters.

Masters

Within this Grand Hierarchy, Masters occupy a unique position. Being Sons of God, they are able to traverse the entire scope of God's creation from Positive to Negative Poles. As the True Light Bearers, they are subject and subordinate to no one except the Supreme Lord God Himself. Hence, they can be viewed as God's chief executives on earth. They come and go at will. Their chief duty is to rescue souls from the maelstrom of the material worlds, taking them to spiritual liberty in the Lord's supreme region. Without Masters all souls would be doomed to circulate within the lower regions of matter, the worlds of pain, tragedy, sorrow, tears and endless birth, death and rebirth.

Why, then, one may ask, don't Masters simply enlighten the world with one sweep of their Mystic God-Wand and eliminate all evil, all darkness? Why don't they eliminate the Negative Power? Because, simply, they act in accordance with God's Divine Will and His Will is that this creation is to exist. It *is designed by the Father for our benefit, to purge us and make us clean, ready for our homeward ascent.* It has its purpose as the Negative Power, its ruler, has his purpose. *All* is under the direction of God whether we understand it or not.

But the fact of Masters being so powerful does raise issues for Satan. If Masters were allowed to come into his domain demonstrating their infinite power, all the soul's in this creation would flock to the Masters, and

Kal would have nothing and no one to rule. Therefore, Masters tell us that God granted three boons to the Negative Power to solve this dilemma. Those three advantages are that 1. Saints could not perform miracles or use supernatural powers to persuade; 2. no one would be allowed to remember his previous life and 3. each soul would be comfortable and content in its present form and condition.

Why no miracles or supernatural powers as the first boon? As Maharaj Jagat Singh states: *nothing appeals to people faster than a show of miracles.*[29] Besides, miracle-making is not the purpose nor hallmark of a Perfect Master. Says Jagat Singh: *When one makes progress spiritually, marvelous powers come to him. One can heal the sick, cure the blind, cast out evil spirits, feed hundreds from one loaf of bread, walk on water, fly in the air and do a hundred thousand such miraculous acts. But there is nothing spiritual in it. This is the result only of a little concentration of the mind in the mental plane. . . But using these powers for personal ends is dangerous. It is playing into the hands of the Negative Power, Kal-the Satan.*[30]

Besides, the teachings of Masters regarding the Reality of God and the fact that one can be God-Realized and escape from this dimension are far more important truths than the mere display of a few petty tricks of the mind, tricks by which a true seeker of the Lord should neither be fooled nor deceived. After all, for all the miracles that Christ performed for the multitudes, how many true disciples did such miracle-making create for him? Are people simply looking for some magic show to thrill them, or are they truly seeking to follow a spiritual path, replete with all the sacrifices such a path demands?

Concerning miracles, one more thought. Incarnations, prophets and other servants of the Negative Power *do* perform miracles to entice souls. But such enticement is designed strictly to entrap and ensnare souls, not liberate them. Saints can do whatever miracles they choose because they are God in manifest form, but their appeal is meant for true seekers of the Lord, not miracle seekers, and the true seekers are those individuals who are committed to eternal and deep Truth, not ephemeral or superficial truth; who are committed to adjusting their lives to accommodate His will, not their own.

Why no memory of one's last life as one of the boons given to the Negative Power? Simply because if we could remember our last life or lives, we would not repeat the same mistakes we continually make and have made in previous lives which keep and have kept us enslaved to Satan, imprisoned in his dark domain. Therefore, it is not important that we learn lessons in this life. It is vital that we find a Perfect Master and *rise above* this life. In true fact, it is critical that we *escape from this life*. Whatever we learn in this life or any life without the Divine Connection of a Perfect Master will be erased at death and 'round and 'round we'll go . . . again and again and again in the Wheel of Eighty-Four.

And why would Kal insist that each soul be content with its present form? Because discontent breeds unrest and rebellion. If a slave is content, he does not ask questions about his life. He simply accepts his life. Content slaves create no problems for their masters. As far as Satan is concerned, he desires to have contentment among his prisoners. God forbid that one of his inmates should ever be discontent! Such a discontented inmate could start a massive rebellion and free all the souls in the entire prison! This is, obviously, not a positive thought which the Negative Power would choose to entertain.

Summary

The Negative Power is the lord of this creation extending up to the second spiritual region of Trikuti. As ruler of the three perishable worlds - physical, astral and causal - he is also called Satan, Lucifer, the Devil, Beelzebub, Dharam Rai [the King Judge], Universal Mind and, of course, Kal. He is the Lord God of the Bible, the Jehovah of the Jews and Christians, the Allah of the Mohammedans, the Brahm of the Vedantists, the god of practically all the world's religions. He is not an equal power of the Supreme Lord but, altogether, a rather low subordinate in the Grand Hierarchy of God's

Universe and, in fact, is just a morsel of God. He rules this creation through the Law of Karma and the laws of nature. Factually, he was created by the Supreme Power, is sustained by Him and carries out His Supreme Will. In the Divine scheme of things he serves God's purpose which is to hold us here, creating a struggle which purges us and makes us strong and fit for our Homeward ascent.

Kal is simply the administrator of this nether universe. As Maharaj Sawan Singh, the Saint of Beas, explains: *The governance of this world is in the hand of Kal and he has so arranged that no soul should go beyond his sphere.*[31] Says Saint Jagat Singh: *Kal does not want a single soul to get even an inkling of what lies beyond him. Through the agency of revealed books, prophets and incarnations, he makes himself known as the highest spiritual stage of development and the maker of all creation, and his law is infallible.*[32] Added to this catalogue of false prophets giving false, deceitful messages, *Satan misleads us by making us worship dead, not living, Saints.*[33] He does everything in his power to keep the soul [entrant] from entering the University of Spirit [the Tenth Gate or Third Eye], what to say about contacting the Word, Shabd, Nam, the Audible Life Stream?[34] Basically, he is just doing his job as ordained by the Supreme Lord.

Yet, our job is to escape his grasp which, in essence, is our greatest spiritual struggle in this world.

Without a Perfect Saint to guide, protect and take us Home, we could not be successful in this struggle or in any escape attempt from this evil Lord of Darkness who rules, ruthlessly, over this land of Satanic shadows, this labyrinthine nightmare devoid of Living Light.

To effectuate our escape from this pejorative prison, we need a Perfect Master. This is obligatory. He is the one who holds the key to our release. He is the one whom Kal fears and even though *the world is a plaything of Kal,*[35] Kal is a mere play thing of God and His Sons - His Perfect Masters who come to rescue us from the clutches of the Negative Power and take us Home to *the Absolute Positive Power, the Lord God Himself.*

Netherland

© Richard Andrew King

This is the land of the Negative Power
where only darkness rules.
This is the land made great with death
where there are no virtue schools.
This is the land where duplicity reigns,
the snare of woman-man;
This is the Dungeon of Darkness.
This is Netherland.
-so-
Enter ye who choose to be
captives of the night;
once within, escape is dim,
and all that is, is fright.

When we step in
this labyrinth den,
anguish fills the air;
moaning, groaning, wailing cries
make it hard to bear;
deceiving, scheming, lying tongues
steal what we own,
and the gravity of the depravity
erases thoughts of Home.
-so-

Enter ye who choose to be
captives of the night;
once within, escape is dim,
and all that is, is fright.

This Devil's lair is fashioned fair
to trap us with delights;
to magnetize our wayward eyes
with streams of wonders bright.
Yet, his Net is intricate;
few escape its thread;
peace is non-existent
with nightmares in the bed.
-so-
Enter ye who choose to be
captives of the night;
once within, escape is dim,
and all that is, is fright.

Killing is the way of all
who live within this realm.
It can't be any other way
with the Devil at the helm.
He has no other purpose
than to rule by wicked sin,
and only those who do succeed
live to worship him.
-so-

Messages from the Masters

Enter ye who choose to be
captives of the night;
once within, escape is dim,
and all that is, is fright.

The greatest of delusions
as we dwell within this den,
is to think that when we die
we somehow go to Heaven.
How slick, how sick
this Devil does deceive,
to offer us this can of trash
and this bag of wind believe.
-so-
Enter ye who choose to be
captives of the night;
once within, escape is dim,
and all that is, is fright.

The alarming ken within this den
is the Wheel of Eighty-Four--
eight million, four hundred thousand forms,
each with a private door;
each with a different body,
each with a different cell,
each with a different outlook
of its private life in hell.
-so-

Timeless Truths for Spiritual Seekers   King

Enter ye who choose to be
captives of the night;
once within, escape is dim;
and all that is, is fright.

The great sad fact of all this talk
is that we're already in,
living in the Darkness,
of the Devil's Dungeon Den;
suffering on the Wheel,
boiling in indigent plight,
and the only way to save the day
is to call His Name by night.

If we do seek His Presence,
if we live by His might,
if we adjust our erring ways
to manifest His Light,
if we disclaim all loyalty
to the Devil's ruling hand,
then there is hope that God Supreme
will save us from Netherland.

But if we don't, then *cest la vie*;
Netherland will be home
for another million ages;
another million lives alone,
and we'll remain in darkness,

Messages from the Masters

wailing in the night,

praying, still, with all our will

for Him to end our plight.

-so-

Seek the Lord, the One Supreme,

and rise into His Sky;

Enter In the Great Within

where you can never die;

dedicate your every breath

to recitation of His Name,

and you will exit Netherland

and win life's greatest Game,

and know, in fact, that Netherland

is the devil's world,

and if you don't escape his claws,

once more you will be hurled

back into the labyrinth

where the hope of life is lost

for millions upon millions

of lives - such is the dreaded cost.

But time _is_ running out;

numbered are our breaths;

if we don't make Connection

with the Lord we'll never rest.

Our true and only lifeline

is the Current and its Light;

if we don't carve our place in it
we <u>will</u> be cast into the night

Of a deep, foreboding wheel
where's the soul's forever tossed
from form to form in agony;
where the truth of God is lost;
where the hope of our Salvation
and the Liberation of our soul
will never be an issue,
for the mind will never know

Within the Wheel's depths
that there is a God,
that there is eternity
for those who seek to trod
the Path of Sound and Light
that is truly liberating,
a Path of Holy Energy
and a Current captivating.

Awake, dear soul; do not neglect
to heed this warning true;
the human form is for Escape,
that's why it's gifted you;
Your time is running out
as you breathe your every breath;
if you don't act now while alive,
you'll live regret in death.

Messages from the Masters

Hell is real. So is the Wheel.
Human life's not ours to choose.
If we don't use it while we can,
Tragically, regretfully, we lose.

So enter ye who choose to be
Disciples of the Right;
once Within, our slavery ends,
and all there is, is Light!

Do not delay; do not avoid;
heed this warning true:
Kabir, the Mystic, utters clear,
"I warn you!"

The Wheel

© Richard Andrew King

Revolving round and round since time began;
eight million, four hundred thousands forms--the plan;
vegetable, insect, bird, fish, animal, man,
create the prison-house of Netherland.

The Wheel exists to captivate the soul;
to keep it steeped in darkness and below
the Realm of Light where it can never know
of its glorious majesty when it is whole.

This wicked Wheel, through pendulum poles,
keeps entities trapped in various hell-holes
of living forms where the spirit never glows,
where darkness rules and Lucifer controls.

Whirling and swirling in negative space,
the Wheel reels--merciless place.
Life and death, at a frantic pace,
create a land of living waste.

No peace exists as the Wheel turns,
as the night enshrouds and the fire burns;
no rest, no joy, as the spirit yearns
to free itself as the Wheel churns.

Messages from the Masters

On and on and round and round,

ceaseless grinding, ceaseless sound

of dying souls--unholy ground,

where ne'r a tranquil soul is found.

Sadly, we think the Wheel's home,

this labyrinthine tomb of catacombs,

where the Mephistophelian metronome

ticks deadly tocks of a Mayan syndrome.

Dead we live in this heap of dung

where Celestial Music is seldom sung,

where the sound of the bell is never rung

except when a prisoner's cell is sprung.

And we all live here in our ignorant bliss,

enthralled with the touch of the Devil's kiss;

the thought of the Word we just dismiss,

too lost in the Wheel to reminisce

of the Land of the Lord where His Godly Grace,

and the luminous glory of His loving face

fill every speck of radiant space,

in realms where bliss is commonplace.

The Wheel, in all of its myriad rooms,

is the dungeon of darkness and tomb of doom

where the soul is trapped in a shroud of gloom

and escape from its grip is never soon

Timeless Truths for Spiritual Seekers   King

unless the soul, being Wheelworn,

and having the Devil's Kiss forsworn,

begs the Lord to be reborn

in the gift of the priceless human form

where escape from the Wheel is ever true,

rising above the realm of Two,

on beyond the Til and through

to a luminous, numinous, rendezvous

with the Lord in all of His Wondrous Light,

embraced and protected by Master Might,

prisoner freed from the horrid fright

and the doom of the Wheel's dreadful night.

Forsake the Wheel and its evil lord,

with his baneful boys and malignant hoard,

and raise the blade of the Master's sword,

swiftly cutting this Nether cord,

this rope that binds you to the Mind,

and renders the sight of your vision blind.

Then, look Within where you will find

the Comforter and His love Divine,

and go with Him. His Laws obey.

His Word will the Devil and his demons slay.

His Light and Sound will guide the way,

and take you Home where His Fortune's lay. . . Forever!

Messages from the Masters

The Devil's Gate

© Richard Andrew King

Deluded by ego, men fall for the bait
of worldliness at the Devil's Gate.
Drenched with their egos through to the bone,
they sail in boats loaded with stone,
fooling themselves of the truth they've known,
drowning in storms before reaching Home.

If man did not the Lord forsake,
there'd be no fear of the Devil's Gate.
But man, so full of self and sin,
happily enters the Devil's Den.
Fooled by deceit and the pride of place,
man rejects the Master's Grace.

He struts himself in peacock form,
denying the Lord and spewing scorn
for all that's holy, pure and chaste--
thus becoming a living waste.
In punishment for his endless spate,
he enters the Wheel at the Devil's Gate.

Devoid of virtue and holy ways,
man's banned Below and forever pays
for his evil allegiance and godly hate -
just recompense at the Devil's Gate.
Perhaps, in millions of Wheeled lives, he'll learn
that those who violate His Edicts, burn!

Bibliography: Chapter Eight

1   *Tulsi Sahib, Saint of Hathras*, J.R. Puri/V.K. Sethi, Radha
    Soami Satsang Beas, 1981 p. 59
2   *Guru Nanak, His Mystic Teachings*, J.R. Puri, RSSB, 2nd
    edition, 1982, p. 236
3   *The Path of the Masters*, Julian Johnson, RSSB, 13th edition,
    1985, pp.232/237
4   *The Master Answers,* Maharaj Charan Singh Ji, RSSB, 1966, A
    347/348
5   *The Path of the Masters*, p. 237
6   Ibid., p. 239
7   *Spiritual Gems*, Maharaj Sawan Singh Ji, RSSB, 1965 L 205
8   *The Science of the Soul*, Maharaj Jagat Singh Ji, RSSB, p.126
9   *The Path of the Masters*, p. 309
10 *Kabir The Great Mystic*, Isaac A. Ezekiel, RSSB, Punjab, India,
    4th edition, 1979 p. 311
11 *Guru Nanak, His Mystic Teachings*, p. 382
12 *Divine Light*, Maharaj Charan Singh, RSSB, 4th edition, 1976,
    pp.73/74
13 Ibid., p. 156
14 Ibid., L 313, p. 283
15 Ibid., L 344
16 *Sar Bachan, Book I: Teachings*, Huzur Swami Ji Maharaj,
    RSSB, Punjab, India, #154
17 *Divine Light*, L 354
18 Ibid., L 316
19 *Mysticism, The Spiritual Path, Vol. II,* L. R. Puri, RSSB, 3rd
    edition, 1964, pp. 133/135
20 Ibid., p. 136
21 *Kabir, The Great Mystic*, p. 129
22 *Divine Light*, p. 111
23 *Tulsi Sahib, Saint of Hathras*, p. 43
24 *Guru Nanak, His Mystic Teachings*, p. 396
25 Ibid., p. 381
26 *The Path of the Masters*, p. 421
27 Ibid., pp. 43/44
28 Ibid., pp. 43/44
29 *The Science of the Soul*, p. 126
30 Ibid., p. 221
31 *Spiritual Gems*, L 199
32 *Science of the Soul* p. 126
33 *Kabir The Great Mystic*, p. 172
34 *Spiritual Gems*, L 114
35 Ibid., L 115

Messages from the Masters

Chapter Nine

SOUL FOOD

The soul is hungry.
Its food is the Current.[1]

I n *The beginning was the Word, and the Word was*
with God, and the Word was God. The same was
in the beginning with God. All things were made
by him and without him was not any thing made that was
made.[2]

This quote from the first chapter of St. John in the
Bible is a concise and beautiful depiction of the reality
of God. Yet, it has generated much confusion and
misunderstanding. When understood in the light of the
teachings of the Saints, however, it becomes crystal
clear, especially when corroborated by one's personal
inner experience.

When we look at this passage, its salient aspect is
that the word, "Word," is capitalized. This is significant.
In literature capitalized words possess a special and

expanded meaning beyond their more mundane and common definition. Thus, because the word, *Word,* is capitalized, we must look more deeply into its meaning to ascertain its exceptional significance.

In this case the word, *Word,* does not merely signify a written word - one composed of simple letters. If *Word* were not capitalized, this would make sense. Unfortunately, the definition of the *Word* has come to be misinterpreted as the written word. But logic tells us that if the *Word* of God could be reduced to mere written words then any one who could read would be saved, their soul liberated and freed from the clutches of this dark world. Furthermore, anyone who could write could change the Word. Simple observation shows us that this is not the case. Millions of people have read holy scriptures in varying languages for millennia but they are still earthbound.

Additionally, if the written word were *the* word of God, then texts in all holy scriptures of every tongue would be identical because the Word of God is constant, it does not change. But holy books do change their texts. Even texts of the same holy teachings in the same language change. If one were to review the many different versions and editions of the Bible, for instance, one would clearly see that words change from publisher to publisher.

For example, take the sixth commandment: *Thou shalt not kill.* In some Biblical versions this reads: *Thou shalt not murder.* The words *kill* and *murder* are <u>very</u> different and they are not interchangeable. *Kill* means to take the life of any living thing; while *murder* implies to many people only the killing only of humans. Thus, there is a huge discrepancy here. The first implies that the killing of all life is a sin. The second relegates such sin only to taking the life of human beings. In clearer words and by this logic it's acceptable to kill as long as one kills animals but not humans. Thus, we have to ask, "Does God's Word have versions of truth, and do sins have varying penalties depending upon which version of His Word, His Truth, it is to which one subscribes?"

Yet, the Bible is supposed to be *the word* of God. If the *Word* of God is changeless, how could two such different definitions exist within the same work? Could God mean that if a person reads one text it is unacceptable to murder only humans but acceptable to kill other living things while, by simply reading a different text, it is unacceptable to kill anything at all? Isn't killing, killing, regardless of the type of life form involved? Furthermore, is God so capricious that His Word can change from book to book, edition to edition, publisher to publisher, race to race, culture to culture, and age to age? Of course not.

In this passage of St. John the word, *Word*, does not signify a written word - one constructed with letters and found in a book. Nor does it reference simply a philosophy or point of view. Saints tell us that the *Word* is something far greater, far more expansive than a mere written word. The *Word*, capitalized, signifies something very different, something much more grand, majestic and all-encompassing as one would expect the *Word* of God to do. Its true meaning, known to all Saints and taught by all Saints, carries an extremely transcendent, spiritual and mystic meaning beyond the minute scope of a mere written word on a piece of paper.

The principle underlying the *Word*, by the way, is not exclusive to Christianity and the Bible. It is common to all religions and spiritual disciplines throughout the world. For example, in Eastern Indian culture the *Granth Sahib*, also called the *Adi Granth*, is a holy book on par with the Bible. In the *Granth Sahib* the *Word* is called "Nam" and "Shabd Dhun." However, in the *Holy Quran* - the sacred text of Muslims, it is referred to as the "Kun." The *Vedas* - Indian holy scriptures - refer to the *Word* as "Nad." In the *Upanishads* the word "Anhad" is used, and Mohammedan Saints have referenced it as the "Kalma." Obviously, because of their different languages, these holy writings use different spellings and appellations to refer to the *Word* but they are *all* referring to the same fundamental essence - *The Voice of God*.[3]

This is exactly what the *Word* is - *The Voice of God*. Saint Kabir, a Perfect Master of Muslim descent says: *The Word is God in dynamic action*.[4] *It is the source of all true spirituality*.[5] Guru Nanak, the first of the Ten Sikh Gurus of India, says that the *Word*, the "Shabd" in his language, *is God's very being and essence. It reverberates in all planes and is the source of all life and the fountainhead of all consciousness. It may be taken as the omnipresent form of God.*[6] He also says: *In the Word is found all rapture.*[7] Notice here that Nanak uses the English version, naming the word as the Word.

Tulsi Sahib, the Great Saint of Hathras, gives us his definition: *Word, Word, say all: listen from where it comes. True Word is transcendent; it is unstruck melody. The unstruck Word is not the word which can be written or read - 'lettered' it may be called. The word which all mankind speaks can be rendered into letters . . . The unlettered Word is indeed transcendent, known only through hints given by Saints.*[8]

The *Word*, then, is not a written word, a 'lettered' word. It is, precisely, a *sound, a melody, a voice.* It is *God in dynamic action, the omnipresent form of God.* Thus, it is something that can be heard, not with our material physical ears, but with the *organs of transcendence* which reside within the human body and are known by all Perfect Mystics.

Maharaj Sawan Singh Ji defined the Word as a *Current* of Divine transcendent energy. He says: *The Sound Current, which is present and audible in everybody, is the way to rise up, go back to our Spiritual Home and meet our Lord.*[9] [It] *is the Royal Road that leads the attention onwards. This Current is life. It is the Essence. It is within us, for us.*[10] *The Sound Current . . . is the grand trunk road between ourselves and the Kingdom of God.*[11] *There is no power on earth or heaven greater than the power of the Sound Current. It is the Primary Power.*[12] *Without it, nobody can go into the higher spiritual planes.*[13] *The Word*, says this Great Master, *is the foundation on which the whole visible and invisible structure of the Universe is resting. Everything has sprung from this Word.*[14]

Thus, we see that the *Word*, as defined by a varied number of Perfect Saints, is much more far reaching than a mere written word. It is God Himself manifested as a primal Sound, as Celestial, Transcendent Music and as a Sound Current.

We can think of it this way. Consider electricity. It is defined as a current of energy and even as an entity in some dictionaries. Entities are living things. Electricity is responsible for much of our technological advancement. Think where we would be without it? Yet, electricity is a *material* current. However, there does exist a *Spiritual* current, a *Transcendent, Living Source* of power that sustains the entire creation. As Sawan Singh says: *the Current is Life. It is the foundation on which the whole visible and invisible structure of the Universe is resting.* As electricity is to the material world, the Sound Current is to the entire creation. Without the Current, there could be no life because *life is the Current*; the Current is *God in dynamic action.*

Furthermore, this *Word* which was *in the beginning*, this *Word* which *was with God* and which, in fact, *is* God, is a *Current*, the most mystical and powerful of all currents and, as Maharaj Sawan Singh Ji says, is the basic nutritional source for our soul, for *the soul is hungry. Its food is the Current.* Hence, this *Word* of God mentioned by St. John in the Bible, this Transcendent, Mystical, Spiritual Current is *Soul Food* for we cannot live without it! As the Current sustains the universe, nay, in fact the whole creation, it also sustains us - the living inhabitants of the creation.

This concept of the *Word* as the Transcendent Voice of God - in fact, as God Himself - certainly elevates it to the august and auspicious level that St. John meant it to have. Written or lettered words do not have intrinsic, transcendent power. The word, *Word*, is capitalized in the Bible because of its truly great significance beyond the finite limitation which it is normally given as it simply being a written cipher. However, the true *Word* has divine meaning and, hence, it is written as *Word* with a capital W.

Attributes

The *Word*, which is *God in dynamic action*, is called the *Name* by Saint Ravidas, an Indian Mystic. *Name* is simply another variation of the Hindu word

Nam. Of this *Name* he says: *It was true in the beginning and shall remain true in the end. It destroyeth all sins and sufferings and is, indeed, the mine of all true Bliss. Nam is the root of all knowledge. Nam is the door to salvation. The one whose heart is occupied by the Lord falls not into the entanglements of the world. Nam is the only means to cross the ocean of the world. Never leave, O Ravidas, the rudder of the Name of God.*[15]

How powerful is the *Name*, the *Word* - true in the beginning; true in the end; destroyeth all sins and sufferings; the mine of all true Bliss; the root of all knowledge; the door to salvation and, most importantly, *the only means to cross the ocean of the world*!

Ravidas continues: *Those who are deprived of Nam are, as it were, living corpses. They will suffer eternal dishonor. They will be regarded as so filthy and defiled that no one would like even to touch them. Despite the glory and grandeur of their life, they will depart empty-handed from this world, failing to achieve the primary objective of their human birth.*[16]

Here we get a strong dose of what it is like for those who do not possess the *Word*, the Holy Ghost, who are deprived of it. They're simply dead - living corpses! Not only this but without the *Word* or Nam they will have to suffer eternal dishonor. Eternity is a long time! Regardless of how great and grand their worldly and material life was, without the *Word* they will have failed

Messages from the Masters

to achieve the primary objective of human life, which is God-realization.

Since the *Word*, the Current, is the nutritional sustenance for the soul, without the *Word* the soul starves . . . to death *and* dishonor. This is why most people in the world are spiritually starving - their souls are hungry for the *Word*, the Current, and the material machinations of this non-spiritually focused world simply cannot feed the soul. The soul *needs* - absolutely, unequivocally, undeniably, irrefutably *needs* - the *Word*, the *Current*, the *Name*, the *Shabd*, the *Audible Life Stream*. It is starving literally to death, and until people awaken to this spiritual reality, they will continue to be lost, confused, distraught, misguided, wanting, lacking and aching for peace, contentment and true Bliss which *only*, as Saint Ravidas says, the *Word*, the *Name*, can give. This is why Ravidas states on a personal note: *God's Name alone is my sole support, my only anchorage. It alone is my life, my vital breath and wealth.*[17]

Kabir, a simple weaver Saint, declares of the *Word*: *I will reveal this secret to the wise: that no one in this whole wide world is saved from the ever-hungry jaws of waiting death except through worship of the True Name of the Lord. All those without the true Name of the Lord are swallowed at the end in the bottomless pit. But the eagle of death is frightened at the very sight of those the Master has attached to the true Name. Kal turns his face away in utter fear of seeing a devotee of the True Name.*[18]   Kabir warns us further: *I tell thee again, remember the Name, else after death thou shalt repent and then it shall be too late.*[19]

Here we see the critical importance of being in possession of the *Word*, its raw power and the consequences dispensed to those souls who do not have it. First, only those who are in touch with the *Word* escape death; in other words, life within the Wheel of Transmigration - the eternal coffin of death and birth. They who possess the *Word* gain eternal life. Those without it *are swallowed at the end in the bottomless pit*! Second, even the Negative Power is deathly afraid of one who is in touch with the *Word,* the Current, Nam and Shabd - he *turns his face away in utter fear of seeing a devotee of the True Name.* Third, a warning - *remember the Name*, the *Word*, or it will be too late to repent when death comes stalking at our door, as it most certainly will.

This knowledge should give comfort to those who have sacrificed their worldly life in pursuit of a spiritual one. Basically, what Kabir is saying is that worldly-minded and worldly-focused souls will be lost in the end; spiritually focused souls will not. This echoes Christ's teaching: *But he that shall endure unto the end, the same shall be saved* (Matthew 24:13).

Therefore, how important is it to live a spiritual life, to turn away from the world and seek God, seek the

Messages from the Masters

Word of God? Every action has a consequence, and spending an entire human existence saturated in pursuit of worldly success, fame, name, wealth, status, prestige, pleasure, comfort, sensual sensation and gratification will bring its consequence which Kabir tells us will be to be *swallowed at the end in the bottomless pit.*

Furthermore, to live *in* and *be of* the world while alive and then try to repent at death in the hopes of being saved from the terror of hell and horror of the Wheel is incorrect thinking. God is not fooled by our silly, infantile chicanery and specious deceit. Death will not bring Salvation, and at the time of death it will be too late to repent for our errant ways of squandering our great human opportunity in worldly pursuits and on worldly accomplishments. Repentance is done while being alive, not while being dead. To wait, to procrastinate, to violate Divine Decree while being free within this human form to pursue God will only create unspeakable consequences for the soul. That's why Kabir warns: *I tell thee again, remember the Name, else after death thou shalt repent and then it shall be too late!* Therefore, to think we can sin for our entire lives and then just before we die affirm our belief in God in order to save ourselves is fallacious thinking. We must have *time* to prove our worthiness to the Lord *before* we get to the end. Hypocrisy will not fool God who knows all. Therefore, we must not delay in transforming our lives to follow the spiritual path if we want salvation.

Nanak says: *Without the Word people wander in delusion. They die only to be reborn over and over again.*[20] If we could only remember! If we could only relive those terrible moments of countless lives in numberless forms when we died gruesome, bloody, terrifying, horrifying deaths at the hands and in the clutching claws of some blood-thirsty predator. If we could only remember the agony and endless, screamingly endless, pain and suffering within the heat and pressure of the womb as each of our new bodies was being formed for entrance into yet another ephemeral material life which would, once again, end in terrorized death. If we could only remember the depth, oppressive intensity and endless sanguine tears of our wailing cries in loss of loved ones to whom we had become inextricably attached. If we could only remember the fear of fear and the heartache of heartbreak. If we could only remember the bitter and despair-filled doom of slavery and being bound in chains by those more powerful, more greedy, more evil than we. If we could only remember the tragic and sorrowful litany of our endless lives in this creation, we would seek the *Word* and never have to be born in *this* world again. If we could only remember. If.

But we can't. It was one of the boons granted to the Negative Power when he assumed governance of this creation that souls would not be allowed to remember their past lives because if they could, they would indeed repent and Satan would have no way to hold them here, to bind them in slavery to him, to keep them wandering from form to form on the Wheel in blind ignorance of the *Word* which alone is their Salvation.[21]   Thus, Perfect Saints like Kabir warn us of impending disaster if we do not seek the *Word*, the *Current*, the *Name*, *Nam* and *Shabd*.   Nanak, too, warns: *Beware, man, lest thou forget and remember not the Name of God!* [22]

So, how do we make contact with the *Word* of God?   How do we come to be in contact with it so we can be eternally saved, so we will not have to roam endlessly from life to life, form to form suffering on and within the horror-soaked Wheel of Transmigration? How do we enter into a spiritual life style?   How do we get the Word?

The Living Master

No man cometh unto the Father but by me.
[St. John 14:6]

The *Word* is life, everlasting life.   As the Bible is an account of one historical Master, Jesus, giving spiritual life to his disciples, so every Perfect Living Master does the same for his followers, his flock.   When Christ told his disciples: *No man cometh unto the Father but by me,* he did not mean 'me' the personality Jesus but 'me' the Master Jesus, the one who was ordained by God to collect specified souls for a specified period of time and return them to God. *Except a man be born of water and the Spirit, he cannot enter into the Kingdom of God* [St. John: 3:5].

Here, says Maharaj Charan Singh, *Christ advises us to get initiated through the Son of the Father and thus get in touch with the Spirit within. That is what he meant by being born again. The day of our initiation is the day of our spiritual birth, and unless we take a new birth - that is, get initiation from a Living Master - we cannot go back to our Father.*[23]

Hence, the *Word* of God must come through a Living Master. In short, it is only the *Living Master* who can impart the *Living Word*, the *Living Energy of God.* Says Saint Jagat Singh: *The Treasure of Nam is within us but the key to It is in the hands of the Guru.*[24] Here we see the word guru is capitalized as it often is. Thus, as with the capitalized *Word*, it also has special significance. The word 'guru' simply means teacher or guide. There are millions of gurus in the world in all sorts of subjects. But when guru is capitalized, it signifies not just any teacher or master but a *Perfect Teacher*, a *Perfect Guide* - a begotten Son of God. A *Sant Sat Guru* is the highest of all Gurus, all Masters.

It is from this Guru, this Perfect Master, that one must get the *Word.* As Maharaj Sawan Singh Ji explains: *A living teacher is needed to school our children; a living doctor to prescribe for our ailments; a living judge to settle our disputes and a Living Master to give us our lost Jewel - the Word.*[25]

Guru Nanak corroborates this: *Without the guidance of the true guru, we cannot find the Name. Without the Name life has no purpose. It is birth and death and regret.*[26] Kabir puts it colorfully yet succinctly: *O you dull-head. Just know this. That without the help of the Master, you will not be saved from this tragedy. This is the game - go to the Master; get the Word and worship the Lord.*[27]

It is imperative to seek a *living* Master, not a dead one. A *Living* Master is the begotten Son of God whom God Himself licenses, so to speak, to impart His *Living Word* to those souls who sincerely desire to return Home to the Father. As the *Word* is the *Grand Trunk Highway*, the *Royal Road* which the yearning soul must travel upon back to the Regal Realm of the Lord, the soul must be placed on the Road, on the Highway, by one of the Lord's specially marked Sons. In effect, the *Living Master is* the *Living Word* of God in the flesh who places spiritual seekers on the road Home. *Living* Masters, as Sons of God, give life through the *Word*. Past Masters, however great, cannot give life - at least not in the *living* sense. Yes, we have their teachings, but because they are not *here in the flesh*, they cannot plug us in to the *Living Spirit*. For that we need a *Living Master*.

Plugging In

This is easy to understand by using the analogy of a light bulb. Until the light bulb is connected to an active living source of energy, until it is *plugged in* to an electrical socket, it cannot emit any light. Until that auspicious moment when the light is actually plugged in, the light bulb is basically dead, inert, inactive. It emits nothing. It radiates nothing.

Each of us is like this light bulb. Spiritually, we're dead. We may be alive as far as the world is concerned but to God and His Word, we're not even close to being alive. However, by the Grace and Goodness of God as manifested through the Perfect *Living* Master, we can get plugged in to the spiritually-charged current of the *Word* and we can, then, radiate light. In truth, we become alive, actually *alive*, and are factually born *again* in the Spirit, the Spirit of His *Word*, His Holy Sound, His Shabd, His Name, His Nam. But all of this is possible only through a *Living* Master. He's the one who holds the secret key to *plug us in* to the *Word* of God.

Maharaj Charan Singh says that when we hear the *Word*, the Sound, the Holy Ghost, the Shabd, we get everlasting life. *We are all dead,* he says, *because we have forgotten the Lord. As far as the world is concerned we are living, but as far as the Lord is concerned we are dead. When we get in touch with that Holy Ghost [or Audible Life Stream, Shabd, Nam or*

Messages from the Masters

Word or whatever name you give it] then we are resurrected from the dead.[28]   It is the *Living Master* who gives us *Life* by connecting us with, plugging us into, the *Word*, the Sound Current of God.

The Path of Nam, remarks Huzur Swami Ji Maharaj, *can be had only by contact with a Saint. But this advice is only for those who are true seekers and not for men of the world.*[29] This passage obviously underscores the sincerity of the seeker. God cannot be fooled and only a true seeker, a person with deeply committed desire to see God and return to Him, will be given the *Word*, i. e., connected to the Sound Current.

Swami Ji continues: *The Lord Himself has ordained that He can be realized only through the Guru. One without a Guru will have no access to His Kingdom. But the Guru must be a perfect one.*[30] Swami Ji Maharaj further elucidates the relationship between the Perfect Master and God by declaring: *The Lord and the Guru are one and there is no difference between them. You will not realize the Lord by worshipping Him directly, but by worshipping and serving the Sat Guru you will realize God.*[31]

How significant, then, is the Perfect Living Master? He and the Lord are one in the same - not in quantity but quality. The Living Master is the wave of the ocean of God - moving, undulating to the Will of God. He is our great and necessary connection to the Word. He is the key to our Salvation. Correspondingly, Maharaj Sawan

Singh Ji says: *The Sound Current is a Wave of the Ocean of Spirituality of which the soul is a drop.*[32]

All Perfect Saints place emphasis on having a *living* Master to initiate souls onto the spiritual path. Written words, whether spoken or read, cannot connect one with the true and transcendent *Word* of God. In this regard Great Master says: *Books give. . . description. . . but do not give. . . experience and knowledge. Description of a thing is not the thing.*[33] This is the hallmark of a *Living* Master: he teaches from *experience - direct, divine, supernal experience of all that is spiritually transcendent and Real.* He may use his intellect but he is not centered in intellect. He is centered, divinely centered, in God. *Living Masters* are the Ph.D.s of Spiritual Science and God-realization. They are the apotheosis of Divine Reality.

Of course the world is convinced that material science knows all or is capable of knowing all. IQ [intelligence quotient] is the god of intelligentsia, which is precisely why they will remain mortal. Sadly, and to their own 'Wheeled' chagrin, worldly scholars, scientists, intellectuals and philosophers will ride the great transmigratory wave into the abyss of Chaurasi just as every other creature will do who does not make the Lord's Name his number one priority in life. Life, in its most elevated and supernal expression, is anchored in the Spirit, not the intellect or its parent, the mind.

Messages from the Masters

Masters are the exemplars of SQ, spiritual quotient. Their subject matter is grounded and founded in the *functional reality of God.* They are spiritual scholars extraordinaire. They do receive criticism from worldly constituents because worldly-minded pundits and intellectuals always try to prove life through *external* means while Masters reveal the Truth of Life based on the *internal experience* of God. But no worries. As Great Master says: *Let people say what they like. To talk of philosophy is one thing. . . but to be a philosopher is another. If a dog walks through a cotton field, he does not come out dressed in a suit!*[34] In other words, it is *functional understanding,* not intellectual scholarship, that supports and proves Reality. And there are educated intellectuals who follow the spiritual path but in spiritual science *there is no difference between the educated and the uneducated. All preference is given to love only. . . Life is made better only through love of the Lord and of Nam.*[35] Intellectualism has nothing to do with being worthy of entrance to His Kingdom.

Initiation and Beyond

What is Initiation? Initiation is that moment when the *Living* Master connects the soul to its *Living* Source, the *Word* of God, the *Living* Current. It is imperative that we have a *Living* Master, not a dead or past master, to connect us to the *Living* Energy of God. It is simply impossible for a dead master to connect us to the *Living*

Radiance of the Creator. From life we get life. We do not get life from death. From that auspicious moment forward, the roots which have been holding the soul to this creation for eons of time, forcing it to wander ignobly on the Wheel of Eighty-Four, are forever severed. The soul's ties to the negative power are also forever severed. At that precise moment the soul is forever connected and protected by the Living Master and officially headed Home, Home to the Lord, back to the heart and hearth of His warm, endearing, eternal love and effusive, radiant and resplendent Bliss . . . forever.

For a spiritual seeker this *is* the Moment of Triumph! Worldly people seek praise, adulation, recognition and validation from the world, its inhabitants, organizations and leaders. Football players, for example, live for the Super Bowl; baseball players live for the World Series; soccer players for the World Cup; tennis players for a Grand Slam; politicians for presidencies; businessmen for treasure chests; actors and actresses for Oscars and intellectuals for collegiate degrees and letters of learning. In achieving their worldly goals, these souls get their rewards, rewards based in and rooted to the world, rewards which will stay in the world when their recipients depart from it.

Spiritual seekers, however, live for God, for the *Word*, and for that one, defining, glorious moment when they achieve the achievement of achievements - Initiation onto the Spiritual Path by a Perfect Living

Saint! It is at this defining moment that God, not the world or its people, honors the God-seeking, God-searching, God-loving soul. In all of creation nothing is more auspiciously and supernally eminent. When God Himself honors a soul by putting him in touch with a Living Master to be returned to the Father forever and thereby releasing him from the prison-house of this world, what more is there of greater value? Nothing. Initiation is *the* ultimate achievement save making that one final step onto the Divine Threshold of the Lord's Immortal Mansion in the ultimate inner Realm. And even that moment is guaranteed at the time of Initiation. Initiation is, therefore, the Divine reception of the Gift of Immortality, and such a gift is reserved, not for worldly people, but for every sincere seeker of the Truth and the *Word* of the Supreme Lord.

Initiation by a Perfect Living Master is *the* greatest moment that any soul can or will experience in its entire existence in this creation. But what then? Is the process of God-realization over? Once a soul is connected and plugged in to the *Word* of God can it sit back on its laurels and bask in the sun of its achievement? Not hardly. The work, the *real work*, is just beginning.

Initiation is the irreversible, official acceptance of the soul into the educational system of the Lord. From that moment onward, inward and upward *progress on the Spiritual Path depends upon purity of conduct and, secondly, upon persevering labor to still the activity of the mind by means of Repetition.*[36] The mind and its voracious appetite for the external pleasures and allurements of the outer world is the enemy. It must be conquered and surpassed. The Path, after all, is the journey of the soul inward and upward in direct opposition to the ever-flowing outward and downward pull and propensity of the mind. As man cannot serve God and Mammon simultaneously, so one cannot travel inwardly and outwardly at the same time either. Remember Kabir's story of the ant carrying a grain of rice and then spied a grain of pulse? She couldn't carry both and was forced to make a choice between the two.

Initiation is the soul's commitment to travel the *inner journey* of God-realization and to turn its back upon the world . . . forever. Once Initiated there is no turning back. Initiation is an irreversible event. This is why Perfect Masters always admonish spiritual seekers to thoroughly investigate the Spiritual Path and be irreversibly committed to it, for once acceptance has been given, the Lord does not allow the soul to reject it. Life is serious business and the activity of God-realization is the most demanding of all.

The educational system of the *Word*, like any educational system, has levels. For a new Initiate, entrance is at the nursery school level. There is much to learn. Much to do. Much hard work ahead. The Reward is there but in order to graduate with a major degree from the *University of the Word*, one must first matriculate through the levels of nursery school, elementary school, intermediate school, high school and college. Upon graduating from this most supernal of universities, one will gain eternal freedom and divine bliss. But it will take time to reach the point of graduation. We've been roaming in the Wheel for millions of lives and eons of time, and in order to reverse the process of our thinking, behavior and instinctual patterns to which we've become accustomed through this interminable and sordid journey, it will take time, and we will have to exercise extreme patience, diligence, fortitude and an indomitable will to succeed. We must be solidly realistic about this because, *For getting the highest thing in life, we have to pay the highest price.*[37] Nothing is free in this world and we do have debts we've been accruing for eons of time, debts that must be repaid before we can go home. As Christ states: *Verily I say unto thee, thou shall by no means come out thence till thou hast paid the uttermost farthing* (St. Matthew 5: 26). But rest assured, once a soul is Initiated by a Perfect Saint, the soul will not fail. The Master is duty-bound to return him to the Lord and so the issue of failure does not arise. Success is a given. That does not mean, however, there won't be any cleansing or scrubbing. Before we can enter the hallowed halls of God, we have to be absolutely pristine pure and to be pure means there's going to be a lot of soap coming our way . . . and even more scrubbing.

The method and procedure regarding the study of the *Word* will be given by the Perfect Master or his representative at the time of Initiation. It is of no use to discuss these matters here. Such a discussion would be inconsequential. What is needed, and that upon which the genuine and sincere spiritual seeker should concentrate, is a purity of life style and the nurturing of an extreme desire to devote oneself to the Lord and His Way, not the world's way. The Lord sees all and knows all. He would never deny any sincere devotee of His Omnipotent Love. When the seeker is ready, the Master will appear to bring the seeker into the fold of the Lord's warm and eternally endearing embrace. Until then, the battle cry is, "Purify, purify, purify and pray to God only for Himself!" As Saint Dadu exclaims: *Hold pure, stay pure and say pure. Take the pure, give the pure.* When God feels the soul is ready, God will then connect Himself to the soul through the Presence of a Perfect Living Master. It is His Way.

Summary

The soul is truly hungry. Its food is the Current. This *Current* is the *Word* of God mentioned by St. John in the Bible and by all Perfect Masters in all tongues in all times. This *Living Word*, this transcendentally charged *Divine Sound Current*, is that power which feeds, nourishes and sustains us. This *Word* is, by other tongues, known as *Shabd, Nam, Nad, Dhun, the Audible*

Messages from the Masters

Life Stream, the Kun and Kalma, the Unstruck Melody, the Sound Current. The written word is not the *Word* of God. We must not be deceived. The true *Word* is the *Transcendent Voice of God.* It resides in all of us and all we need do to experience it is live a spiritual life devoted to God and seek a *Perfect Living Master* who can connect us to God's *Perfect Living Word.* When this happens through the process of spiritual Initiation, we will have accomplished the ultimate achievement. We will be going Home, forever. Therefore, what we must do first, if not already Initiated, is find a Living Master and beg him for *the Word.* We should do this even if it takes lifetimes. Then, once Initiated, we must do our spiritual work according to his instructions and directions. Eventually, we will step across the Divine Threshold of Immortality and our soul, which was hungry, will never, ever, be hungry again!

The Word

© Richard Andrew King

Reading, writing, 'rithmatic,' and scholarly acclaim
will never give of us knowledge of the Secret of His
Name.
Nothing flowing from the Mind or intellects absurd,
can ever bring *experience* of the Lord's Resplendent
Word.
The *Word* is not a written thing printed on some page;
nor is it a spoken art gushing from some sage.
The *Word* is His Transcendent Voice--intrinsic, primal
Sound,
emanating from His Core and resounding all around
with the Unstruck Music of His Love, the Vibration of
His Being,
of which the intellect's incapable of seeing.
Only by the soul is His *Word* heard, perceived,
and it is the *Living Master* who insures that we believe,
by connecting soul to Source and attaching us to Him,
opening our Inner Eye to His *Word* voiced *Within*.
Intellect cannot do this, no more than blind men see.
The *Word* is inexplicable to intellectuality.
Only soul is Godly made to hear His Holy Sound,
which is why the human body walks on Holy Ground,
the Ground of His Perfection and His Experience;
the Ground of Pure Devotion and Ethereal
Transcendence.

Messages from the Masters

So do not look to books or rumors overheard

to find the Magic Power of His Omniscient *Word*.

The *Word* exists *Within* and *Within* we must go

to experience the Pristine Truth and ultimately know

that the *Word* is His Vibration; His Essence found

Within.

To capsulate this Living Truth. . . the *Word* Divine is

Him!

Catch the Current

© Richard Andrew King

If we would catch the Current,

we must, first, reach the Eye;

in the Eye begins the Current

as it flows to Higher Sky.

The Eye contains the Current;

the Current holds the Sound;

the Sound, by nature, carries us

to Regions where abound

untold sights and mysteries

beyond the ken of man,

spectacular amazements

true travelers understand,

those who work to lift themselves,

with Grace, up to the Eye

to catch this Royal Current

where one cannot deny

the total Fact and Truth of God,

and man's Divinity,

but man must catch the Current

to discern this Certainty.

So catch the Current if you can,

if you want to run His Race;

but, first, you must beseech the Lord

to give to you His Grace,

the Grace which flows from His great Love,

Messages from the Masters

through the Living Master's hand--

the Keeper of the Current,

so catch Him. . . if you can!

Serious Business

© Richard Andrew King

Life is serious business.
A truth we can't deny –
a truth made more the poignant
when we die.

Life is serious business.
Our Salvation is at stake,
and to waste one precious moment
is the greatest, grave mistake.

We've been given life within this form,
within this human frame,
to Realize the Lord Within
by contacting His Name.

If we choose not to follow Him
and play away instead,
we can't be optimistic
of our future when we're dead.

God lives within this body coil,
as Perfect Saints agree.
If we're to gain His Kingdom,
we must live Righteously.

Messages from the Masters

No meat, no drugs, no alcohol,
no sex unless we're wed.
It may seem bitter medicine,
but soon we will be dead,

and the way we lived our life
will determine where we go –
higher in His Spirit,
or drenched in woe below

in the furnace of the Wheel's forms
where wailing cries abound
from the torture of the Devil's fire
in the Devil's Nether Ground.

Life is serious business.
We must be ever wise.
There will be consequences
for the way we live our lives,

And we must know, He's watching us
to see the choices that we make,
to see if we are worthy
from this world to graduate,

to move on in the journey
of our soul returning Home;
if not, we may be banished
to lower fields to roam

Timeless Truths for Spiritual Seekers   King

from form to form in endless toil
upon the Wheel in distress,
all because we disbelieved
that life was serious business.

And to think we rise to Heaven
when we die is foolish thought
if we don't put in effort
for our effort is the Plot.

No one gains diplomas
by wishing on a star.
No one gains Salvation
ignoring God afar.

No one gets a Ph.D.
without hard work for years.
Likewise, God is Realized
by yearning sweat and tears.

It's just not fair to grant degrees
unless the work is done.
The University of God
rewards Divine Devotion –

loyalty, allegiance,
commitment to His Laws,
a lifetime spent in living pure
and cleansing all our flaws.

Messages from the Masters

Why should the Lord be gracious
and grant us Life Divine
if we spend life ignoring Him
and wasting precious time?

God expects our effort
if we're to Merge with Him.
There are no instant purchases
in quest to enter In.

God is not a man and can't be fooled
by slippery slights of mind.
His criteria for graduation
lie in acts Divine.

By praying Him with empty tongue
to save our soul at death
is useless act of ignorance
and wastes our precious breath.

If we chase Him devotedly,
at death our soul is saved;
but if we turn our back on Him,
it's Hell beyond the grave.

Life is serious business,
and time is running out;
and, by the way, earth's riches,
to God, have zero clout.

Timeless Truths for Spiritual Seekers   King

What works with God is love,
devotion to His Cause,
living Right and Purely
and honoring His Laws.

Violation of this form
and the life with which we're blessed,
will not gain us His Kingdom,
for life is serious business.

Make your choices now,
but be careful how you choose.
If you deny His Way of Life,
without a doubt, you'll lose.

God did not give us human form
to squander in our days
of earthly life and living
in search of earthly praise.

God gave us life and body
of human form to save
our errant souls from bondage
and the horror of the grave,

to lift our soul past Heaven
to Realms of Peace and Bliss,
to Merge with Him Forever
in the Love of His Sweet Business.

Messages from the Masters

So, be mindful of your life,
grateful, and do not miss
the opportunity of human life,
for life is serious business!

Never may it come again,
and it's scurrying away.
Be about His Business
and don't let ignorance betray

the Gift of Gifts of creatures
born into this earth –
the precious, priceless, human form
with its precious, priceless worth.

Life is serious business.
Be careful as you trod.
The actions that we make today
lead us to Hell or God.

It's true we have a choice
on how to live and why,
but, remember, life is passing
and soon we'll have to die,

and death is not an end
but a door which opens wide
to either Hell or Heaven
when we pass to the other side!

Timeless Truths for Spiritual Seekers   King

So, my friends, be ever wise.
Betray no Future with a kiss.
Miss not this opportunity
of honoring His Sweet Business!

Take not this life for granted.
Trust Saints and all they know.
Your Life is serious business.
Come Home and save your soul!

Bibliography: Chapter Nine

1   *Spiritual Gems*, Maharaj Sawan Singh Ji, Radha Soami
    Satsang Beas, L 44
2   *Bible*, St. John, 1:1 - 3
3   *Spiritual Gems*, L 130
4   *Kabir The Great Mystic*, Isaac A. Ezekiel, RSSB, 4th edition,
    1979, p. 162
5   Ibid., p. 330
6   *Guru Nanak, His Mystic Teachings*, Professor J. R. Puri,
    RSSB, 2nd edition, 1982, p. 81
7   Ibid., p. 264
8   *Tulsi Sahib, Saint of Hathras*, J.R. Puri/V.K Sethi, RSSB,
    1981, p. 123
9   *Spiritual Gems*, L 73
10 Ibid., L 145
11 Ibid., L 117
12 Ibid., L 95
13 Ibid., L 66
14 Ibid., L 195
15 *Guru Ravidas: Life and Teachings*, K.N. Upadhyaya, RSSB,
    1982, pp. 56/57
16 Ibid., p. 149
17 Ibid., 49
18 *Kabir The Great Mystic*, p. 328
19 Ibid., p. 257
20 *Guru Nanak, His Mystic Teachings*, p. 261
21 *Spiritual Gems*, L 2
22 *Guru Nanak, His Mystic Teachings*, p. 452
23 *St. John - The Great Mystic*, Maharaj Charan Singh Ji, RSSB,
    p. 17
24 *The Science of the Soul*, Maharaj Jagat Singh Ji, RSSB, p. 49
25 *Spiritual Gems*, L 104
26 *Guru Nanak, His Mystic Teachings*, p. 261
27 *Kabir, The Great Mystic*, p. 127
28 *The Master Answers*, Maharaj Charan Singh Ji, RSSB, A. 8
29 *Sar Bachan, Book 2: Sayings*, Huzur Swami Ji Maharaj,
    RSSB, # 87
30 Ibid., # 92
31 Ibid., # 90
32 *Spiritual Gems*, L 33
33 Ibid., L 34
34 Ibid., L 54
35 Ibid., L 160
36 Ibid., L 90
37 *Teaching of the Gurus*, Professor L.R. Puri, RSSB, 1973 p. 89

GLOSSARY

Adi Granth	Indian holy text; also known as the Granth Sahib; compilation of the writings of Saints.
Astral Plane	The next plane of existence above the physical and below the Causal plane.
Audible Life Stream	See "Word"
Audible Life Stream	See "Word"
Baba Jaimal Singh	19th Century Saint; founder of the Dera, a spiritual community in Northern India; worldly profession was in the Indian military. . He was the second Perfect Master in the Radha Soami line of Perfect Saints.
Brahm	The second spiritual region known as. Trikuti.
Causal Plane	The plane of existence above the physical and Astral planes.
Celestial Music	See "Word"
Chakra	Spiritual-cosmic energy vortex within the human body. There are eighteen chakras taught by Saints, twelve of which are primary.
Chaurasi	Chaurasi (Wheel of Transmigration) is the spiritual-cosmic configuration housing the 8,400,000 forms, bodies and structures into which our soul is deposited, incarnated and reincarnated. Same as the Wheel of Eighty-Four.
Current	The Audible Life Stream; the pure energy of the Supreme Lord.
Dharam Rai	Another name for Kal; King-Judge

Dhun	See "Word"
Granth Sahib	Indian holy text; also known as the Adi Granth. compilation of the writings of Saints.
Guru Nanak	Perfect Saint of India in the 15th and 16th Centuries; first of the Ten Sikh Gurus; principal contributor to the Granth Sahib (Adi Granth); contemporary to Kabir and Ravidas; known as the Great Saint of the Punjab; his worldly occupation was a storekeeper.
Holy Names	Secret names given at Initiation by a Master to his disciple connecting the disciple with the Master's power.
Initiation	The connecting of a soul to its Source, God, by a Perfect Living Master.
Inner Master	The Supreme Lord who dwells inside us.
Kabir	Perfect Saint of Muslim descent of the 15th and 16th Centuries and one of India's greatest Masters; a weaver by worldly profession. Contemporary of both Nanak and Ravidas.
Kal	The Negative Power and magistrate of this plane. Also known as Satan, the Devil, Lucifer, the Prince of Darkness, Dharam Rai and Mammon.
Kalma	See "Word"
Karma	Sanskrit word for *action*. Karma is the inexorable law of sowing and reaping, cause and effect, compensation and adjustment, action and reaction, which is eternally operating in this dimension.
Lakh	One lakh equals 100,000.
Lucifer	Literally, "light-bringing." See Kal

Maharaj Charan Singh	Perfect Saint of the 20th Century; leader of the Radha Soami Faith based at Dera Baba Jaimal Singh in the Punjab, India from 1951 to 1990; collegiate degrees in Arts and Law; during his tenure, the Teachings of the Saints expanded worldwide to over one million souls. He was the fifth Perfect Master in the Radha Soami line of Perfect Saints.
Maharaj Gurinder Singh	Perfect Saint and current (2008) leader of the Science of the Soul faith. He is the sixth Perfect Master in the Radha Soami line of Perfect Saints.
Maharaj Jagat Singh	Perfect Saint of Indian in the 20th Century; chemistry professor by profession; also called "Guru Ji." . He was the fourth Perfect Master in the Radha Soami line of Perfect Saints.
Maharaj Sawan Singh	Perfect Saint of the 19th and 20th Centuries; referred to as *Great Master*; born in Punjab, India; an engineer by profession; served time in the Indian army; Sant Mat, the teachings of the Saints, expanded globally under his Mastership; he initiated the first Americans into the Radha Soami Science of the Soul. . He was the third Perfect Master in the Radha Soami line of Perfect Saints.
Maulana Rum	A Moslem Saint of Persia; also known as Rumi.
Manmukh	Devotee of the mind; one absorbed in the mind rather than the spirit. Its opposite is a Gurmukh - one absorbed in God.
Master	Son of God incarnate, the manifest form of the Lord; the Word made flesh; also referred to as Living Master, Perfect Master, Perfect Saints, Guru, Sat Guru, San Guru. Their life purpose is to liberate souls from this world and take them Home to the Lord.
Maya	Illusion; the force which operates with Kal,

the negative power, to entrap and enslave souls in the Wheel of Transmigration.

Nad	See "Word"
Nam	See "Word"
Physical Plane	The plane of existence in which we currently exist. It is below the Astral and Causal planes of this dimension.
Pind	This worldly dimension.
Radha Soami	Lord of the Soul
Ravidas	Perfect Saint of the 15th and 16th Centuries in India; a cobbler by earthly profession; contemporary of both Kabir and Nanak. Other names for Ravidas are Ramdas, Raidas, Ruidas.
Reincarnation	Incarnate means to take a form, a body. To reincarnate means to take a body again. The process of repeatedly incarnating, i.e., taking on a different form.
Rumi	A Moslem Saint of Persia; also known as Maulana Rum
Sant Mat	The teachings of the Saints
Sat Lok	The highest spiritual region.
Sat Sang	Spiritual discourse literally meaning *true association.*
Satguru	A Perfect Saint who teaches spiritual truth; also spelled, Sat Guru.
Satsangi	A disciple of a Perfect Living Master.
Science of the Soul	Spiritual Path that connects the Soul to its Source, God. Worldwide in scope, it is led by a Perfect Master who resides at Radha Soami Satsang, Beas, India.

Shabd	See "Word"
Shabd Mystics	Perfect Masters, Keepers of the Keys of the Word (Shabd) of God.
Silver Cord	An appendage which attaches the soul to the body. When the silver cord is cut, the life force of the individual is severed and the physical body dies, but if the cord is not cut, the person does not die.
Sound Current	See "Word"
Spiritual Path	The path of the Spirit, of energy and light, not matter; the royal road Home.
Spiritual Salvation	The release of the soul from this dimension and its re-establishment in its true Home with God.
Surat Shabd Yoga	Spiritual science of the Sound Current taught by Perfect Masters of the Science of the Soul (earlier known as the Radha Soami Faith)
Swami Ji Maharaj	Renowned Indian Saint of the 19th Century and founder of the Radha Soami Faith; taught the yoga system of the Sound Current; Patriarch of the Radha Soami line of Perfect Masters. . He was the first Perfect Master in the Radha Soami line of Perfect Saints.
Ten Sikh Gurus	Masters whose writings comprise the *Granth Sahib,* a holy book of the Sikhs, the first of whom was Guru Nanak followed by Gurus Angad, Amar Das, Ram Das, Arjan Dev, Har Gobind, Har Rai, Har Krishan, Teg Bahadur, Gobind Singh. The time span of these Gurus was from 1507 to 1708.
Tenth Door	The Third Eye in mystic teaching; the entrance to the inner worlds. Gateway to the Lord. It is exclusive only to the human body.

Third Eye	Also known as the Tenth Door or opening through which the soul passes en route to the inner regions. It is located slightly above and midway between the two eyebrows of the human body.
Til	Another name for the Third Eye.
Triloki	The Three Worlds: Earth Plane, Astral Plane and the Causal Plane.
Trikuti	The second spiritual region known as Brahm.
Tulsi Sahib	19th Century Saint; born into the royal family of the Peshwas; son of the King of Poona; known as the Great Saint of Hathras and Dakhani Baba (Sage from the South). He was the first Saint to use the term, *Sant Mat* to describe the teachings of the Saints.
True Name	See "Word"
Unspoken Melody	See "Word"
Unstruck Melody	See "Word"
Wheel of Eighty-Four	Also called Chaurasi and the Wheel of Transmigration. It is a construct of 8,400,000 forms into which the soul can incarnate. The human body is the most prized form within the Wheel.
Wheel of Transmigration	Same as Wheel of Eighty-Four
Word	God's very being. God in dynamic action, the source of all true spirituality; the Voice of God referenced by different names in different religions. It is also known as the Logos, Shabd, Nam, Nad, Kalma, Dhun, Sound Current, Audible Life Stream, Celestial Music, Unstruck Music and Unspoken Melody.

CATALOGUE OF POEMS

FINAL NOTE:

If you have an interest in the teachings and writings of Saints, you can find information at the following two links:

1. RSSB.org (stands for Radha Soami Satsang Beas)
2. ScienceOfTheSoul.org

There you will find many books by various Saints in multiple languages—all exist in service to your Divine Being and spiritual success.

RICHARD ANDREW KING – BOOKS
RichardKing.net/books & Amazon.com

The King's Book of Numerology Series (KBNS)

1. *The King's Book of Numerology: Volume I – Foundations & Fundamentals*
2. *The King's Book of Numerology 2 (II): Forecasting – Part 1*
3. *The King's Book of Numerology 3: Master Numbers*
4. *The King's Book of Numerology 4: Intermediate Principles*
5. *The King's Book of Numerology 5: IR Sets – Level 1*
6. *The King's Book of Numerology 6: Love Relationships*
7. *The King's Book of Numerology 7: Parenting Wisdom – Numerology & Life Truths*
8. *The King's Book of Numerology 8: Forecasting – Part 2*
9. *The King's Book of Numerology 9: Numeric Biography, Princess Diana*
10. *The King's Book of Numerology 10: Historic Icons*
11. *The King's Book of Numerology 11: The Age of the Female – Volumes 1 & 2*
12: *The King's Book of Numerology 12: Advanced Principles*

Numerology Books Published Separately

The Age of the Female – A Thousand Years of Yin (KBN11)
Your Love Numbers – Discovering The Secrets of Your Life, Loves & Relationships (KBN6)
Destinies of the Rich & Famous – The Secret Numbers of Extraordinary Lives (KBN10)
Parenting Wisdom for the 21st Century – Raising Your Children By Their Numbers To Achieve Their Highest Potential (KBN7)
Blueprint of a Princess – Diana Frances Spencer, Queen of Hearts (KBN9)

Non-Numerology Books

Karma-The Definitive Guide to the Supreme Law of this World

Messages from the Masters – Timeless Truths for Spiritual Seekers

The Black Belt Book of Life – Secrets of a Martial Arts Master

The Karate Consciousness – From Worldly Warrior to Mystic Master

Parenting Wisdom – What to Teach the Children (Part 2 of KBN7)

The Age of the Female II – Heroines of the Shift (Part 2 of KBN11)

The Galactic Transcripts

99 Poems of the Spirit

27 Delusions of Mankind

To order books, go to

RichardKing.net

Amazon.com

or other major online

booksellers and retailers

CONTACT

Richard Andrew King

PO Box 3621

Laguna Hills, CA 92654

Rich @ RichardKing.net

Notes:

Notes:

Notes:

Notes:

www.ingramcontent.com/pod-product-compliance
Lightning Source LLC
Chambersburg PA
CBHW060004100426
42740CB00010B/1397